Budget Brides

By Di Kivi

Lifetime Books, Inc.

This publication is designed to provide accurate and authoritative information in regard to the subject matter covered. It is sold with the understanding that the publisher is not engaged in rendering
legal, accounting, or other professional service. If legal advice or other assistance is required, the
services of a competent professional person should be sought. *From A Declaration of Principles jointly
adopted by a Committee of the American Bar Association and a Committee of Publishers.*

Library of Congress Cataloging-in-Publication Data
Kivi, Di, 1964-
        Budget brides / Di Kivi.
        p. cm.
        ISBN 0-8119-0873-9 (paper : alk. paper)
        1. Weddings--Planning. 2. Weddings--Costs. 3. Finance, Personal.
     I. Title
     HQ745.K58   1998
     395.2'2--dc21   98-3552
                                                         CIP

Interior Design by Vicki Heil
10 9 8 7 6 5 4 3 2 1s

Table of Contents

Introduction ix
Why I wrote this book for you

Chapter One—You're Getting Married 1
Don't let the wedding of your dreams become a financial nightmare

Chapter Two—Planning 5
So where do you start?

Chapter Three—Knowing Your Budget 15
The serious stuff

Chapter Four—Pre-Wedding Get-Togethers 23
Let's party!

Chapter Five—Choosing The Venue 31
Location, location, location

Chapter Six—Invitations & Announcements 41
Putting the word out

Chapter Seven—Clothing 51
And the bride wore . . .

Chapter Eight—Flowers & Decorations 65
Deck the halls

Chapter Nine—Photographs & Video 79
Lights, camera, action!

Chapter Ten—Transportation 93
Get me to the church on time!

Chapter Eleven—The Reception 97
Eat, drink and be merry

Chapter Twelve—Honeymoons 113
Should last a lifetime

Chapter Thirteen—The Ceremony 119
Time to say "I Do"

Chapter Fourteen—Real Life Budget Brides 135
How we did it

Appendix 147
Useful telephone numbers, addresses and people to talk to

To Arno, with all my love.
I'd marry you all over again, again!

Acknowledgments

There are many people whose help, support and love have made this book possible. I thank them all from the bottom of my heart, but my deepest gratitude must go to some very special people:

- ♥ All the *Budget Brides* who shared their wonderful experiences with me, especially Lois, Kathleen and Christy.
- ♥ Janet and John Friauf, for letting me use their wedding vows (which made me cry while I read them)!
- ♥ Lois Hobart, for being such a terrific teacher, mentor and friend.
- ♥ Sandra Fentiman, who unknowingly got me started on this book!
- ♥ Katrina Patterson, for daily sanity checks (sorry about your phone bills, Ron)!
- ♥ Ann Usher, for her beautiful and original illustrations.
- ♥ Everyone at Lifetime Books, Inc. and National Book Network, especially Callie Rucker (enjoy your wedding, Callie)!
- ♥ The International Women's Writing Guild and the Saratoga Writer's Circle.

Above all, my most heartfelt thanks go to Arno Kivi, my husband, for his unwavering belief in me, for giving me the chance to live my dream, and for the sheer joy with which he fills my life.

Introduction

Why I Wrote This Book For You . . .

When my husband and I planned our own wedding, we both held strong views about saving for our future (we still do!) and did not want to become railroaded by the wedding industry into spending more than we could comfortably afford on our one income. At the same time, this was our wedding and we wanted something special!

Together with a friend, I started the round of bridal stores. One day was sufficient to convince me that enough is enough! The only dress I even remotely liked cost more than our entire budget for the day!

My next stops were the library and several book stores. My initial excitement at finding some books covering the subject of low cost weddings waned rapidly as soon as I read them! Yes, I am sure a bride could save plenty by making her bouquet out of nylon pan scrubbers — but was that the image I had of my wedding? I don't think so! I wanted a classy wedding with a beautiful dress, a bouquet of roses, guests sipping champagne, a glorious frosted cake, photos, video, the first dance . . . yes, I wanted it all. Now all I had to do was find out how to achieve this small miracle!

I longed for an honest, "no false promises" guide to help me hold the wedding of my dreams on our tiny budget — and that is exactly why I have written this book to help *you* have a fabulous day, with all the trimmings you could wish for!

—*Di Kivi*

. . . .

CHAPTER ONE

You're Getting Married . . .

Don't let the wedding of your dreams become a financial nightmare

So, you are getting married! Congratulations! I bet your feet haven't touched the ground yet.

Now that you are ready to start planning your dream wedding, why miss out on having everything you always wanted even though you know you cannot afford anywhere near the average $20,000 cost of a wedding? This book is going to show you how you can have it all — for less than many brides pay for their dress. It is not intended to be an instruction manual, telling you to *do this* or *do that*, but a guide to help you make your own choices. The key is compromise — you will need to practice it in marriage, so why not start now?

1

These days, more and more of us are paying for our own weddings. Even if our parents are footing the bill, few of them can afford thousands of dollars without dipping into their savings. Is it fair to expect them to? Many of us are marrying later (I had cruised happily past the big three zero), some for the second or even third time, and have financial commitments such as mortgages, car payments or even children. This all means that we have less money to spend on a wedding day.

Having a tight budget, for whatever reason, does not mean you have to miss out. By all means, go to the City Hall if that is what you want, but if your dream wedding includes sweeping down the aisle in a fairytale dress followed by huge party for all your friends and family, then I say 'go for it!' — this book will show you how.

Why Should The Wedding of Your Dreams Become A Financial Nightmare?

When they say a June bride is always a bride, it shouldn't be because it takes forever to pay for her wedding. The adjustment to married life can be tough enough, without starting out under a cloud of debt.

Just like me, I am sure you have heard all too many horror stories from couples who can not afford to put a deposit on a home because they spent too much on their wedding. Or worse, couples who are still paying for the event on their fifth wedding anniversary. Let's face it, weddings are expensive.

Statistics show that couples are marrying later and in many cases, especially a second marriage, feel responsible for the cost of their own wedding. But with a mortgage, car payments and many other financial commitments, how many of us can afford the average $20,000 cost of a wedding? And remember, that is the *average* cost.

For every wedding that costs less, there is one that has cost thousands more!

How This Book Can Help You

With a little hard work, imagination, and a lot of fun, you will be amazed by what you can achieve. By following the easy to understand steps included in this book you will:

♥ ♥

Be focused on the true significance of the wedding: the marriage service.

Learn how to plan a budget and stick to it, using the budget sheet included.

Practice mental exercises to envision your 'perfect' wedding.

Find thousands of money-saving tips and suggestions for every aspect of the wedding.

Share the personal experiences of other 'real life' budget brides who have succeeded in planning weddings that are still being talked about.

♥ ♥

Whether you dream of floating down the aisle in a fairytale dress or exchanging your vows in an exquisite outdoor setting, start believing that you can do it. Let me show you how, no matter how tiny your budget!

Share Experiences

Not only will you have the opportunity throughout this book to learn from the experiences of budget brides, but you can join us at our website and share your own story. We would love to hear from you. Tell us your success story, share your suggestions or ask for advice. You can reach us at: http://members.aol.com/bdgtbrides.

Have Fun!

Planning a wedding can become stressful, especially if you are struggling to keep within a budget. The best advice I can give is to remind you to relax and have fun.

You are about to share your life with someone you love with all your heart. Your wedding is the beginning of this life; a celebration as you exchange your vows and become husband and wife. Enjoy it!

. . . .

CHAPTER TWO

Planning . . .

So where do you start?

*J*would like you to try a little mental exercise. Find a relaxing place (your favorite armchair in the sun, a hot tub with scented bubbles — anywhere will do, as long as it is legal), close your eyes and let your imagination run wild. Concentrate on these points:

- ♥ the ceremony
- ♥ your dress — probably the most beautiful dress you will ever have a chance to wear
- ♥ the bridal party — how many attendants would you like?
- ♥ the reception

What do you see? How do you imagine your dream wedding? Keep a note of anything you think would make it special. Write down *everything*, however crazy and outlandish it may seem at the time.

Where do you see the ceremony? In a church or a rose garden, perhaps. Maybe you have always dreamed of getting hitched in a hot air balloon. What does your dress look like? Do you imagine a sexy, sophisticated shift dress or a Cinderella gown (don't forget what happened to Cinderella, and she did not exactly have a huge budget!). What is your favorite flower? Color? Music? What about the reception?

Do you envision an informal buffet where everyone mingles, a romantic restaurant or a formal, sit-down dinner in a hotel? Do you prefer 20 guests or 200? Will there be music and dancing?

Go ahead and repeat this exercise as often as you like until you have a really clear idea of the sort of wedding you would like. If there is any part you are not sure about, try the same exercise with your fiancé, your mom or your best friend. They may have some great ideas.

Getting Started

Now you are ready to start planning in earnest. Keep the list of your dreams and ideas handy as you bring your mind firmly back to earth for now; it is time for a reality check. You know you are on a tight budget, so forget about a sit down dinner for 500 of your closest friends, at a plush hotel on Central Park! To make the planning easier for yourself, follow these four rules:

1. Know Your Budget

Most wedding magazines or books will tell you that the first thing you need to do is either plan your guest list or set the date. In this book they both get pushed back; top billing goes to the budget. This is because your budget will influence so many of your choices. Until you know exactly how much you can afford to spend, you cannot make any of your other decisions. Your budget can even dictate your wedding date — hotels are often cheaper off-season, churches come ready decorated at Christmas.

Knowing your budget and sticking to it is so important, I have dedicated an entire chapter to it.

2. Organize Yourself

Buy yourself a three-ring binder, a set of dividers and a pack of loose leaf paper.

Choose the paper that already has holes punched in it; you are much more likely to keep your folder organized if you do not have to keep hunting out a hole punch. This folder will become your best friend over the next few months, so keep it with you wherever you go!

Mark the dividers as follows:
- My Dream Wedding
- Budget
- Calendar
- Ceremony
- Reception
- Invitations/Announcements
- Clothing, Flowers
- Photographs/Video
- Miscellaneous
- Guest List/Gift List
- Telephone Numbers/Addresses

You will want to use each section like this:

♥ In section one, "My Dream Wedding," file any notes you made during your imagination exercises. List all the ideas you have, even the extreme, expensive or outrageous ones!

♥ The budget section is self explanatory. Keep your budget sheet in here (an example budget sheet is shown in this chapter). Any receipts or written quotes should be kept in this section, too. Staple or tape them to a full sized sheet or punch holes in a large envelope and store them in there.

♥ The calendar (an example is shown at the end of this chapter) will show you what needs to be done, when or by whom. Check each listing off as it is completed.

♥ Under ceremony, file all the information you have collected regarding the marriage ceremony itself. For example, if you plan to write your own vows, keep a copy here. If your wedding is taking place in a church or synagogue, file all the details of the service here.

♥ As with the ceremony, file all the information you have collected pertaining to your reception. For example, file your menu and drink list, the name of the band playing, if you have one, and seating arrangements. Have you seen any examples of great locations? File them here.

♥ The invitations/announcements section will hold samples of invitations and copies of newspaper announcements you may wish to duplicate and make your own.

♥ Clothing will probably be your biggest section. File pictures of wedding dresses you like, bridesmaids' dresses, groom's clothing and anything that the groomsmen may wear. You will want to include headdresses and veils, too, if you plan to wear one.

♥ Next come the flowers. It is a good idea to collect pictures of bouquets and floral arrangements that catch your eye. You will have a clearer view of how they fit in with the wedding theme.

♥ In the photographs/video section, gather together ideas of groupings for the photographs, whom you would like in each picture and anyone you would like to have interviewed on the video. Do you have any pictures from weddings you have been to where you really liked the pose? Keep them in your file. Don't forget to make a note of who will be doing the video or taking the photographs.

♥ Miscellaneous is the easiest — if it does not fit anywhere else, this is where you file it!

♥ The guest list/gift list serves two purposes. Divide your sheets up into four sections by drawing lines from the top to the bottom of the paper. In the first column list the guest's name and address, the second column is for their response (yes/no), the third column is for the gift they give and the last column is for you to check off when you have sent a thank you letter. Not only will you have a list of all your guests that you can mark off easily when you receive their RSVP, but you will have their names, addresses and the gift they gave handy for when you send out thank you letters.

♥ Finally, the telephone numbers/addresses section will be filled with all the important contact details you will need, for example the priest or rabbi, the florist, the caterers. It would also be useful to list the telephone numbers of anyone helping out with the wedding planning — you will be amazed how many times you need to call them.

3. Set Your Priorities

Decide early what is most important for you and your fiancé. For example, if you love dancing, you may want to spend more on the music than, say, on the food.

List all the points of your wedding in order of priority. What means more to you, what is less important? For example:

Top Priority — the ceremony. You are happy to spend most of your budget here as the setting you like is fairly expensive.

Mid Priority — the clothes for the bridal party. The wedding dress you wear is still important but not as significant as the ceremony itself.

Low Priority — the reception music. You both have two left feet, hate pop music and would rather listen to classical CDs.

Forget It — flashy transportation. You have no desire to waste half your budget on a limousine for a five minute drive.

If this were the case in your priority list, your finished list may look something like this:

1. Service/Venue
2. Wedding Ring(s)
3. Ceremony Flowers/Decorations
4. Wedding Dress
5. Number of Attendants
6. Number of Guests
7. Photographer
8. Wedding Cake
9. Reception Venue
10. Reception Catering
11. Flowers/Decorations for Reception
12. Music for Reception
13. Video
14. Transportation to Service/Reception.

You will want to allocate a larger part of your budget to anything at the top of the list and will not mind cutting back on some of the things lower down. Your priority list can be as long and detailed as you wish. The more detailed it is, the easier it will be for you to allocate your funds.

4. Have FUN!

The best part! Who says planning your wedding should be stressful? Too many books talk about how frightening it is and how much you have to do. Yes, you have a lot to do; much more than the bride who has money to burn. In fact, you will probably never work so hard in your life! But, by putting some energy and passion into it, it will be fun; I promise you. I recommend that you follow my example. When I planned my own wedding, I threw away all the books (keep this one — you will need it!) and decided to relax and enjoy myself. It ended up being one of the most joyous and positive experiences of my life; I felt in full control throughout.

By enjoying the experience of planning your wedding, not only will you arrive for the ceremony feeling in control (OK, we all lose it at the last minute, but that is excusable), but your fiancé, friends and family will thank you for not putting them through months of pre-wedding hell!

Planning Calendar

As Soon As Possible:

- ❑ Do your mental exercises to find your idea of a fantasy wedding.
- ❑ Figure out your budget. Know exactly how much you have to spend.
- ❑ Make your priority list — choose the style of wedding that you and your fiancé want.
- ❑ Check out locations for the ceremony and reception. Make reservations as soon as you decide.
- ❑ Reserve the officiant — priest, rabbi, judge, etc.
- ❑ Prepare your guest list.
- ❑ It is never too early to start gathering ideas for your dress.

Nine to Six Months Before:

- ❑ Decide who will do your photographs, video, catering, flowers, music, etc. Ask for their help, or reserve their services if you are using a professional.
- ❑ Talk to anyone else who is playing a significant role in the wedding.

❏ Decide on your dress.
❏ Pick out clothing for your attendants.
❏ Choose what the groom and groomsmen will be wearing and make arrangements.
❏ Make a gift list or register with a store.
❏ Start to think about your honeymoon.

Three Months Before:
❏ Make your invitations or have them printed.
❏ Choose your wedding ring(s).
❏ If you have any guests traveling long distance, find accommodations for them.

Two Months Before:
❏ Send out the invitations.
❏ Confirm any arrangements or reservations you have made.
❏ Arrange transportation to the ceremony and reception.
❏ If you are buying, making or borrowing your dress, arrange for final fittings. Try everything on and have a trial run with your hair and make up.
❏ Select the menu, especially if you are self-catering and choose the wedding cake.

One Month Before:
❏ Arrange blood tests (if required) and marriage license.
❏ Change your name on any necessary documents, e.g. your passport.
❏ If you are having a DJ or band at your reception, give them a list of your favorite songs, including the all-important "first dance."
❏ If you are having taped music, record enough cassettes for the reception.
❏ Discuss poses with the photographer.
❏ Discuss the video with whoever will take it.

Two Weeks Before:
- ❑ Give the caterer final numbers.
- ❑ If you are self-catering, prepare any dishes that can be frozen.
- ❑ Make a schedule for everyone participating -- both the wedding party and anyone helping with the food, photographs, video, transport, etc.
- ❑ Double check everything.
- ❑ Enjoy a few pre-wedding parties or showers.

The Day Before:
- ❑ Finish preparing food for the reception, if you are self catering.
- ❑ Pick up the cake or finish making it.
- ❑ Make the flower arrangements and bouquet.
- ❑ If you can have access to the reception venue, decorate it.
- ❑ RELAX!!

This is just an example of a planning calendar. You will need to make your own individual calendar, according to the type of wedding and reception you are having and how much time you have to organize it.

CHAPTER THREE

Knowing Your Budget . . .

The serious stuff

The first and most important thing to discuss with your fiancé is your budget. Before you do anything as far as actual planning is concerned, even setting the wedding date, you need to know exactly what your budget is and how long it will take you to save for it. When you know how much you have to spend, stick to that figure. To help you keep track of your budget throughout the planning of your wedding, I have included a simple budget sheet at the end of this chapter. Please go ahead and adapt it to suit you and your fiancé, if you like.

Remember to keep your budget realistic. The idea of this book is to help you plan a wonderful wedding without going into debt or paying more than you can afford. Whether you are paying for your own wedding or are parents who want to give your daughter or son a special day, *Budget Brides* is here to help you to plan the event from start to finish, guiding you every money saving step of the way.

Although I have written this for couples with a very tight budget, there are hundreds of money saving ideas included that will help anyone planning a wedding, no matter how much they can afford to spend. I have personally used many of the ideas and suggestions given, either at my own wedding or at weddings I have coordinated, both in the United States and Europe. Throughout the book, and in the chapter titled *Real Life Budget Brides,* other brides share the ideas and success stories of their own weddings. Believe me, when the day comes, no one will have a clue how little you paid.

♥ . . . . ♥
Tip: Dropping the spend, spend, spend mentality keeps the focus on the true significance of your wedding. Your wonderful day is, after all, the beginning of your wonderful life together.
♥ . . . . ♥

If you have families helping to pay the bill, the following is how most etiquette books suggest you break down the cost.

Bride and her family pay for:
- Invitations and announcements
- Ceremony, including venue, music, flowers, etc.
- Bride's dress, veil, accessories and 'going away' outfit
- Groom's ring
- Flower arrangements for the ceremony and reception. Bouquets for the attendants and flower girls
- Wedding photographs and video

- Reception, including catering, drinks, music and any decorations
- Transport for the bridal party to and from the ceremony

Groom and his family pay for:
- Marriage license, blood tests (if required) and officiant's fee (priest, rabbi, judge)
- Groom's outfit
- Bride's bouquet
- Boutonnières for the groomsmen, corsages for the mothers
- Honeymoon — if and when you decide to take one
- Rehearsal dinner
- Bride's ring

Attendants pay for:
- Their own clothing, including shoes and accessories

Seems a little unbalanced, doesn't it? In the case of the budget bride, and any other bride for that matter, I firmly believe that this is one tradition that should be forgotten! It is unreasonable, unfair and out of date. If your families offer financial help in any way, thank them and accept their contribution towards *any* part of your wedding — as long as they can comfortably afford it. Knowing our guests as we did, my husband and I were delighted when his parents offered to buy all the drinks for our wedding reception.

Using Your Budget Sheet

When you have agreed on how much you have to spend, make up your budget sheet and file it in your planning folder. Start at the top with your total budget, then deduct any fixed costs. These fixed costs will be the cost of marriage licenses, blood tests (if required), church, synagogue, clergyman, Justice of Peace and anything else you cannot legally do without. Should you need copies of birth certificates, this expense should be included, too. Anything with a fixed price needs to be deducted at this point.

When you have taken out your fixed costs, you will see exactly how much you have left to play with. Now go back to your fantasy list and decide what is most important to you. This is the time to make up your priority list, as I described in Chapter Two. I would recommend that you and your fiancé get together on this as you may well have conflicting views of how you allocate your money. Talk about your lists until you reach a happy compromise between the two of you. Is it more important to you that you have a lot of guests? Does your fiancé want a champagne only reception, which would, obviously, effect the number of guests you could afford to invite? Is there a particular restaurant that you would both like to use? Allocate a larger percentage of your budget to anything with a high priority — and remember that you will have to cut back somewhere else.

As an example, this is how my husband and I worked out our list, from highest to lowest priority.

♥ **Service/Location.** Although this was the area where we were prepared to spend the most, we decided to hold the service in a glorious, lakeside rose garden, which we were able to use free of charge. A judge officiated for his standard fee.

♥ **Bride, Groom, Best Man and Matron of Honor Clothing.** At the time, my husband was serving as an active duty military officer and chose to wear his dress uniform (and very handsome he looked, too). I have always enjoyed dressmaking and was able to make my dress and veil, as well as a dress for my attendant. The best man wore his own suit.

♥ **Wedding Rings.** We chose matching, plain gold bands, which we bought in our local mall, with the money my grandmother sent as a wedding gift.

♥ **Reception.** With the exception of our wedding cake, which came from a supermarket bakery, I prepared all the reception food in advance. My husband's parents provided more than enough cases of champagne, wine and beer to keep even our thirstiest guests satisfied! We hired champagne glasses for a very low cost. The reception started in our apartment with speeches, toasts and a meal, followed by dancing at a local nightclub —where we were given free admission. I guess they don't get many groups dressed in full wedding regalia, in Texan cowboy bars, these days!

♥ **Flowers.** Flowers for the service were provided free of charge by Mother Nature, with a little help from the gardeners. For my bouquet, I bought a dozen white roses from my local supermarket, which my Godmother arranged and tied with ribbon to match my dress. In my hair, I wore a rose and freesia corsage, which I attached to a plastic haircomb. I made boutonnières by tying a small ribbon around the stem of single white rosebuds.

♥ **Photographs/Video.** We wanted the photographs to be "natural" so decided not to have professional pictures taken. Instead they were taken by a friend who was an excellent photographer and had all the equipment needed. A video camera was passed among the other guests, several of whom briefly lived out their Hollywood fantasies!

♥ **Music.** During the service and early part of the reception, we played a selection of our favorite classical CDs. Later, in the nightclub, the DJ was delighted to announce our marriage and play a special request for our "first dance."

As you can see, our priority list was fairly brief. The rose garden where we held our service was on the grounds of our apartment complex, so we did not need to make any allowance for transportation. We were even able to walk to the nightclub a couple of blocks away.

When you have agreed on your priority list, write up a master copy and put it in your planning file with your completed budget sheet. Now that you have done the hardest part, let's get on with the fun side of the job!

♥ *Budget Sheet* ♥

A. Total Budget: $_____
(how much you have to spend)

B. Fixed costs: $_____
(list each fixed cost)

C. Remaining (A-B) $_____
(how much you have left to split between
everything else)

D. Non-fixed costs:

Invitations/Announcements	$_____
Bride's outfit	$_____
Groom's outfit	$_____
Wedding ring(s)	$_____
Flowers/Decorations	$_____
Photographer	$_____
Video	$_____
Transportation	$_____
Reception venue	$_____
Food	$_____
Drinks	$_____
Wedding cake	$_____
Music - reception	$_____
Misc. costs (e.g. hair stylist)	$_____

E. Total non-fixed costs (D) $_____
(Should be equal to or less than C)
(If this figure is less than C, congratulations —
you came in ahead of budget!)

. . . .

CHAPTER FOUR

Pre-Wedding Get-Togethers

Let's party!

*W*hat better excuse for a party than to announce that you are getting married! The thought of an upcoming wedding is guaranteed to put most people into the party spirit, and as the enthusiasm builds, so will the number of get-togethers.

There is a serious benefit to pre-wedding parties, though. It is the perfect opportunity to introduce families and friends, from both sides, *before* the big event, giving them a chance to get to know each other first.

Here are some suggestions for pre-wedding events that you may like to consider. Please remember that, although these parties can be great fun, none of them are critical to the wedding. If they don't fit into your budget, leave them out!

ENGAGEMENT PARTIES

For the Families

The first engagement party is traditionally hosted by the bride's parents. Cocktails, a formal dinner at a restaurant or club, or a family dinner at home are all great ways to do this. The bride's father will, at the appropriate moment, toast his daughter and soon-to-be son-in-law, who he will welcome as a part of the family. The soon-to-be son-in-law will then respond by thanking him, his daughter and the whole family.

Of course things are not always that simple these days! When parents are divorced or living a long distance from you, it may be impossible to host a traditional engagement party. If this is the case in your situation, don't worry. These are the nineties, and, although good manners are as important today as they have ever been, outdated rules of etiquette are not. If either set of parents, or permutation of them, wishes to host an engagement party for you and any of your family or friends, enjoy it!

For Your Friends

An engagement party with your friends need not be formal at all. It could take place in a bar, where you all meet for drinks after work. At an appropriate moment, one of you can announce the engagement. You may prefer to do it the way my husband and I did. At a bar we often visited, the disc jockey announced our engagement for us.

If you would like to host a dinner, cook it at your home or soon-to-be home. It will show your friends exactly what you do or don't have in your house and give them an endless supply of ideas for shower gifts or wedding presents.

WORKING PARTIES

Start with a group of relations (mother, sisters, aunts, grandmothers, even include your soon-to-be in-laws) and your closest friends, and hold a *brainstorming* session. In a relaxed environment, get everyone present to chip in with ideas. These ideas should cover every aspect of your wedding, from the invitation style to what food to serve. Keep a note of every idea — and as people relax, more so after refreshments, some ideas may become quite far-fetched. Don't worry, though, if you particularly like one of these ideas, most can be adapted to fit your style and budget.

If you are planning to do most of the organization and work for your wedding yourself, you will need to plan several "working parties." These will be for groups of relations or friends that you can rely on to help out with wedding tasks such as sewing, cooking, running errands, etc. Always be sure to offer some food and drinks, even if it's just pizza and sodas, as a "reward" for your helpers.

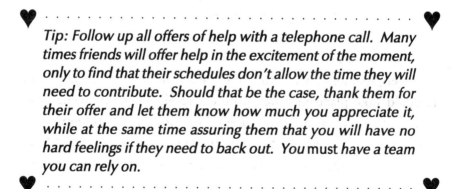

Tip: Follow up all offers of help with a telephone call. Many times friends will offer help in the excitement of the moment, only to find that their schedules don't allow the time they will need to contribute. Should that be the case, thank them for their offer and let them know how much you appreciate it, while at the same time assuring them that you will have no hard feelings if they need to back out. You must have a team you can rely on.

Catering

If you are self-catering, host a buffet party. To obtain menu ideas, host a pot-luck supper, and ask each person invited to bring a dish which they feel they prepare the best. From these, you can select your buffet menu. At the party you can decide what to serve and allocate responsibilities.

Invitations

Get together with your artistic friends — and don't rule out those less artistically inclined, they can help too — and design your invitations. Do you know anyone with beautiful handwriting who could write the envelopes? Are you using stamps or ribbons to decorate the invitations (*see Chapter 6*)? Are any of your friends great at drawing maps and giving directions, which will be needed for out of town guests? Perhaps you just need some help putting everything into the envelopes and sticking on the stamps.

Flowers, Decorations and Favors

Get all your family and friends to offer suggestions for flowers, decorations and favors. If you are not using a professional florist, do you know anyone with a talent for flower arranging? Maybe they can just do the table decorations? Are you planning to use flowers or candles or something completely different for your tables? See what suggestions everyone comes up with and try them out to see how they look.

Favors are easy to make and are generally expensive to buy! How difficult is it, for example, to tie three sugared almonds wrapped in a piece of lace with a ribbon? All it takes is time. With a good working party, you could make hundreds in one evening! Perhaps you prefer to give something unusual as a favor. A bookmark printed with a favorite poem, together with the bride's and groom's names and the wedding date, is a popular variation. Again, by working together, these can all be made in an evening.

Sewing

If anyone on your guest list is a seamstress, either a professional or a talented amateur, she may be willing to volunteer to sew your dress, your bridesmaids' dresses or flowersgirls' dresses, as a wedding gift for you. I have seen this carried out numerous times, very successfully. The results can be quite beautiful —particularly as everything is made with love.

Tasting

Now comes a fun part! Sampling the food and tasting the different beverages, both alcoholic and non-alcoholic, that you have chosen to serve at your reception. This is something both you and your fiancé will enjoy. Why not make a game out of it? Try blindfolding everyone before they start sampling.

PARTIES FOR THE WEDDING PARTY

Bridesmaids Party

This is a get-together, hosted by the bride for her attendants. It is your last chance as a single woman to spend a night "with the girls" and the perfect opportunity to thank them for all the work they have done (of course they helped in the working parties!) and for being there to support you during one of the most important events of your life.

This party could be in the form of a brunch, a luncheon or an evening party. Anything is acceptable. It is also the perfect time to give each of your attendants the thank you gift you have bought for her.

Bachelor Parties

Over the years the bachelor party has degenerated into an orgy of heavy drinking and, well, you know what else! This does not have to be the case, though, and nor should it be.

The bachelor party is hosted by either the groom's father, brother or best man. It is most commonly held in the evening and should take place at least two or three days before the wedding, as you can usually guarantee that heavy drinking will play a role. The last thing you want is a hungover groom who barely knows what is happening during your wedding!

And don't forget, the drinking should always start with a toast to the bride!

♥ .... ♥

Tip: If the bachelor party absolutely has to be the night before, be sure to find some reliable hangover cures. If all else fails, try what in England is called "biting the hair of the dog that bit him." Roughly translated, it means give him a drink to cure the hangover! It may sound a little odd, but it works!

♥ .... ♥

SHOWERS

Bridal Showers

Bridal showers can be hosted by a relative or friend, though it is more usual that they are hosted by an aunt, sister or best friend, rather than your mother. The guest list should include any women who will be invited to the wedding. Guests of honor, aside from the bride, will be the mothers of both the bride and groom.

Pretty much anything goes as far as a bridal shower is concerned and it should be a relaxing evening, away from all the organization of the wedding.

If more than one shower is to be held, for example, if both your family and work colleagues arrange one, guests who attend both should be discreetly told not to bring gifts twice.

His 'n' Hers Showers

As grooms become increasingly involved in the planning and organization of their weddings, his 'n' hers shower are rising in popularity. Guests will be the attendants, from both sides, together with close male and female friends.

Theme Showers

Increasingly, couples have set up their own homes or a home together before they get married. If this is the case, they will usually have many of the items normally given as shower gifts — in duplicate if they have separate homes! In situations such as this, a theme shower is often a better idea. A theme shower could cover anything from the couple's hobbies to everything needed to redecorate a room. Here are some suggestions of themes and appropriate gifts:

- Home Improvement — *paints, household tools, any Do-It-Yourself accessory.*
- Garden — *seeds, garden tools, gardening gloves, terra-cotta flower pots (perhaps with the wedding date painted on).*
- Kitchen — *replace old kitchen appliances.*
- Hobbies — *if the couple collects something, such as a particular style of ornament, add to their collection. If they are interested in photography, give rolls of film, developing gift certificates, etc.*
- Redecorate a room — *supply anything needed from wall coverings to floor rugs to linens.*
- Around the Clock — *allocate a time of the day to each guest, who then brings something appropriate. For example, 7.00 a.m. - an alarm clock; 11.00 a.m. a set of coffee mugs, 7.00 p.m. a bottle of wine and a corkscrew, and so on.*

- Bring a Bottle —*for those who need help to stock the bar for the wedding reception. Each guest brings a bottle of liquor towards the reception as a "cover charge." Per bottle, the cost is very low; for 20 or 30 bottles, being paid for only by the couple getting married, the cost is astronomical!*

BEFORE AND AFTER

Rehearsal Dinner

The rehearsal dinner is usually the last get-together for all the bridal party and immediate family members. It follows straight after the wedding rehearsal. This party can be anything from an informal buffet at home to dinner in a restaurant.

Afterglow Breakfast

If you have guests who have traveled a long distance to celebrate your wedding, show them that you appreciate this by arranging an afterglow party. This need be nothing more than agreeing a time to meet for breakfast the morning after the service. Even if you are leaving immediately for your honeymoon, go ahead and set up an afterglow breakfast. All the guests will have had a chance to meet the day before and will have plenty of beautiful memories to share.

. . . .

CHAPTER FIVE

Choosing The Venue

Location, location, location

As in buying real estate, the three most important things to look for when deciding where to hold your wedding are location, location and location. When you visualized your dream wedding, where did you see it take place? Is it important to you that the service be held at your church or synagogue? Or do you prefer something less traditional? Beside a lake? An apple orchard in the spring? The town park? A rose garden in the height of summer? Be sure to choose somewhere that suits your personality as well as your budget.

Is there somewhere that you both love, such as the beach or a historical building? Do either of you belong to a sports club with clubroom facilities? Your choice of location will sway the answers

31

to many of your other decisions — and will help to make your choices easier. Consider holding both the ceremony and reception in the same place. Not only will this save you money but also time — and none of your guests can get lost on their way to your reception!

We are fortunate in this country to have few restrictions on where we can marry. Depending on your budget and creative imagination, there is no end to the options you have. Does either your family or your fiancé's family have a particularly beautiful garden? Or a lawn big enough for a tent? Hold your wedding in a garden and you can pretty much cancel out a flower budget. Let's face it, who can beat Mother Nature as a florist? Again, if you choose a beach, forget about buying expensive flowers. All you will need is the bride's bouquet and boutonnière for the groom.

When my husband and I married, we chose to have our ceremony and the start of our reception in a small rose garden, beside a lake. We paid nothing to use the garden, which belonged to the apartment complex where we lived, and the gardeners worked particularly hard to make everything look its best — even clearing up after the ducks! The combination of white roses and green shrubs matched the colors I had chosen for the wedding party and looked spectacular. The only additional flowers I bought were for my bouquet, the boutonnières/corsages — a total of two dozen white stem roses from the local grocery store — and two white freesia corsages that the maid of honor and I wore in our hair.

Perhaps you, too, live in an apartment complex with a club house or communal garden. Does your town have an attractive park? Do you live in the country? Does your church or synagogue have a hall or function room? Is there a favorite restaurant you would like to use?

Your choice of location is a major decision and one that needs to be made as soon as possible. In many cases, the time of year will effect your choice. Many hotels are cheaper off season. Perhaps you are a skier. How about a supermodel style wedding on a mountainside?

If you have set ideas as to where you would like to hold your ceremony and reception, your choice will be easier. If not, let your imagination run wild. Have fun with all the ideas. They will not be as crazy as they sound. Don't just think of *places* you love, think about *things* you love, such as a particular style of music. If you love jazz, is there a jazz bar or restaurant nearby? If they have live music, you will have a band playing for free.

Below is a list of suggested locations. All of them can be used for very little cost, many of them would be free of charge altogether. Check to see what is available in your local area.

When you choose your location, reserve it and enter the cost into your budget sheet.

- ♥ Apple orchard
- ♥ Bar/nightclub
- ♥ Beach

♥ Church or Synagogue
♥ City Hall
♥ Club house
♥ Historical monument
♥ Hot air balloon
♥ Hotel
♥ Lakeside
♥ Museum
♥ Private chapel
♥ Private garden
♥ Private house
♥ Restaurant
♥ Rooftop garden
♥ Rose garden
♥ Ski mountain
♥ Town park
♥ Vineyard/winery

These are just a few suggestions, some of which I will describe in greater detail later. The time of year will also dictate when and where you hold your wedding and reception. Outdoor locations may well be suitable year round in the southern states, where the weather can be relied upon to cooperate. An outdoor wedding where I now live, upstate New York, would be limited to June, July or August — unless you choose a snow setting. Also, remember that bars or nightclubs are not be suitable for children.

Bar or Nightclub

Advantages:

☝ If you choose one that has music, you and your guests can dance the night away without the expense of hiring a band or DJ. I would suggest selecting one where you know they play 'catchy' music that will be familiar to most of your guests.

☝ Usually the cover charge to visit a bar or nightclub with music and dance space is fairly low. Some more accommodating clubs may even waive this cost. When you discuss the reception with the manager, be sure to reserve adequate tables for all your guests and ask if you can decorate them.

☝ You can supply drinks such as beer, wine and soda, and let guests order stronger drinks, if they choose, at their own expense.

Disadvantages:

☞ It is unlikely that you will be able to serve food unless it is supplied by the bar or nightclub. You may find that the only food you can serve is the wedding cake.

☞ You will not have sole use of the venue, although most people will respect that you are holding a private event and keep their distance.

☞ The noise level can be very high, which dampens conversation and makes toasts and speeches difficult.

Church or Synagogue

Advantages:

☝ Many churches and synagogues have reception rooms attached. These can be rented for little or no cost.

☝ Kitchen facilities are available for catering.

☝ You will be able to go in ahead of time and decorate.

☝ As the reception is at the same place as the marriage ceremony, it avoids having guests drive from one venue to another.

Disadvantages:

☞ Many churches or synagogues will not allow you to serve alcohol on their premises. If your heart is set on a champagne toast, you may wish to choose a different venue.

☞ Some reception rooms can look a little stark. However, if this is the case, you can put up decorations, if this is permitted.

Club House

Advantages:

👍 If you are fortunate enough to live in an apartment complex with a club house, you can often have private use of the rooms, free of charge. At the most, a nominal fee will be charged.

👍 Depending upon where you live, many open up onto a pool area, which can make a very attractive setting.

👍 You can provide the food yourself or have an external caterer prepare it. There are no restrictions.

👍 In general, serving alcohol is acceptable and much less costly when you supply it yourself.

Disadvantages:

👎 Sometimes the club room can be small. I have seen both large club houses with tables and chairs provided and small, homely clubrooms, better suited to a lunchtime buffet.

👎 You may find that there are restrictions on the times you can use the club house, for example, if the complex offices are in the building, it may be open to the public during certain required hours.

Hotel

Advantages:

👍 You can hold both the ceremony and reception at the same location. Only one room will have to be decorated and your guests will not have to travel between venues.

👍 Some hotels offer discounts and special incentives, such as free hors d'ouevres and cake, in the low season. Check with each individual hotel for their policy.

Disadvantages:

👎 You will be limited to using the hotel's catering staff to serve food and drinks. The expense can add up.

Lakeside Garden

Advantages:

- This is my personal favorite! The setting can be absolutely beautiful. Many parks have lakes, whether they are man made or natural. Most of them will have an area that has some paving — you don't want to be standing in mud.

- You can set up tables for a buffet and have your reception at the same place, immediately following your ceremony. Check with local authorities about liquor laws. You may need a temporary license to serve alcohol. Soft drinks would pose no problem.

Disadvantages:

- As with any public spot, you will find that you become a point of interest. If you don't object to kindly onlookers or passers-by calling out their good wishes, this should not be a problem.

- As I mentioned above, you will need to check for the laws regarding serving alcohol in public parks.

Private Chapel

Advantages:

- You can purchase an all inclusive package at private chapels. Although the minister, flowers, music, photographs and video are usually included, you should check with each chapel to be sure. Some will also include a certain period of time in a garden for toasts and cake cutting.

- An all inclusive package takes all the stress out of planning, as everything is done for you.

- There are several companies that run all inclusive wedding/honeymoon packages in places such as Jamaica. These will include a vacation on a beautiful tropical island along with your wedding. This type of package is much more suited to a couple who prefer to keep their wedding small and personal. Guests would probably be limited to immediate family or less.

Disadvantages:

🍃 As the time in a private chapel is restricted, you may feel a little rushed. If you pick a busy time of the year, you may find that as you come out, the next couple is waiting to go in.

🍃 With all inclusive wedding/honeymoons, you may have to stay for a certain period of time to fulfill any of the local legal requirements.

Private Garden

Advantages:

👍 No restrictions whatsoever with what you serve for food and drinks, as well as no time limits. This is an extremely versatile setting, if you have a family member with a large enough garden to accommodate your guests.

👍 Tables, chairs, linen, glasses, dishes, flatware, etc. can all be rented at a reasonable cost. Call different rental agencies and shop around. There are bargains out there!

Disadvantages:

🍃 You may have a large number of guests and only one or two bathrooms. Be prepared to have people walking through the house to use them — and be sure to stock up on toilet tissue!

🍃 Depending upon where you live, you may not be able to rely on the weather. If the garden is large enough, rent a tent or canopy. This gives a wonderful festive air and can be decorated to match your wedding colors.

Rooftop

Advantages:

👍 If you live in a big city and have limited access to parks, but prefer an outdoor wedding, a rooftop is the answer. The views are superb.

Disadvantages:

- Be careful if serving alcohol — you don't want anyone falling off!
- Rooftops can get very dirty. You will need to spend a considerable amount of time — and energy — cleaning. You will also need to supply screens or plants to cover more unsightly areas.

Ski Mountain

Advantages:

- No matter how old you are, snow rarely looses its magic. All ski mountains will have lodges, often with blazing log fires, and bars. Many, particularly the smaller, more intimate ones, will allow you to bring in your own food. Check with the director first.

Disadvantages:

- It can get cold for guests if you have your ceremony outside on the mountain. Be sure to warn them so that they can dress accordingly.
- Lodges can get crowded and noisy, especially at lunchtime. Choose a time when less people will be around. Some small mountains are closed one day of the week. See if you can rent the lodge then.

CHAPTER SIX

. . . .

Invitations &
Announcements

Putting the word out

*T*he chances are, no sooner has the groom-to-be got up from his knee, that you will be on the telephone to your mom, your best friend and just about everyone else in your address book! Those you cannot call, you send a letter to. Your mom is so excited, she tells all her friends. They, in turn, tell anyone else who may know you. And so the grapevine spreads! Everyone will hear the news quickly enough, without you and your fiancé spending a dime on announcements. Ask yourselves how many people actually read the announcements anyway!

Here is a perfect example. My neighbors were married recently. I had known they were getting married for several weeks before I read their announcement in the local paper — which caught my eye from the bottom of my cat's litter tray! Is that where you would like to see yours? It is exactly where many of them end up!

Of course, if you have set your heart on an official announcement of some sort, there are plenty of ways to do this economically.

ANNOUNCING YOUR ENGAGEMENT

Newspaper Announcements

♥ Check with the local papers where you and your fiancé live, some offer local residents a free announcement.

♥ Ask about shorter announcements. For example: *Mr. & Mrs. John Brown are delighted to announce the engagement of their daughter, Elizabeth Jane and Mark Philip Black.*

♥ If you or your fiancé are in business locally, send your announcement as a press release.

Some papers have a set format they will ask you to use. They will often ask for the name of the bride and groom, both sets of parents, the date of the wedding, names of attendants and background information about the couple, such as where they went to school, where they work, etc. If the paper charges by word or by line, these can become expensive. Only give the information you are willing to pay to have printed.

On-Line Announcements

Many internet services offer a free website for each sign on name. Use your website to make a worldwide announcement! If you have access to a scanner, include a picture of yourselves, too. If you don't, try office supply stores or copy centers, who can scan for you.

Your website announcement can be as long or short as you choose. There is no format for an announcement of this type — so have fun and make it up as you wish!

Printed Cards

These are usually sent out after the wedding and announce that the marriage has taken place, rather than at the time of the engagement. If, however, you prefer to send out official announcement cards, try printing them yourselves. You will find ideas of how to do this later in the chapter.

Invitations

The invitations can be a great source of savings for the budget conscious bride. How high are they on your priority list? The style of wedding and number of guests you wish to invite will help you choose the type of invitations you use.

If you are holding a small, intimate wedding, for example, you may decide to have your invitations professionally printed, or perhaps handwritten by a professional calligrapher (who will usually charge by the hour). If you are hosting a reception for 50 or more guests, you may want to consider do-it-yourself invitations, printed on a laser printer, or trying one of the discount mail order services available.

Do-It-Yourself

Nowadays, we all have access to a computer and printer, either at home, at work (ask permission from your company first, though!), at a library or at one of the many office supply stores or copy centers around the country. If you are not comfortable with using a computer, don't be afraid to ask for some guidance. Both libraries and copy centers will have staff on hand who will be happy to show you what to do. If you prefer, take a friend along who can help.

Both laser and bubble jet printers give excellent quality print and will give a professional finish. Be sure to use laser compatible paper, though, if you are using a laser printer. Laser quality sheets of invitation cards are readily available, in a variety of sizes and designs, from stationers and copy centers nationwide. Usually there are two or four invitations per sheet, which, after printing, you divide up. I bought a pack of 50 invitations with envelopes in the corresponding size for less than $10!

Discount Mail Order

There are numerous discount mail order companies offering affordable, professionally printed invitations. Look in the back of bridal magazines for their telephone numbers and addresses.

♥ Order catalogs from as many mail order services as possible, so that you can compare their prices, designs and service.
♥ Check for minimum quantities. You don't want to order 50 invitations if you only plan to invite 25 couples!
♥ Avoid the extras. Why use two envelopes? Do you really need reply cards?
♥ Have your invitations printed with the service *and* reception details.
♥ Skip the reply cards and put the response information on the invitation card, too (common practice in many countries).

Stationers

Some stationers now have equipment to produce invitations in-house. Cards come in various sizes and designs and are priced accordingly. You simply pick out the design you like and the appropriate wording, and they will print them for you. Your order can be completed within 24 hours. Do check for layout costs and minimum quantities, though, as these can push the price up.

Professional Printers

Shop around among local printing companies. You will find their numbers in your area's yellow pages or by looking for advertisements in your local paper. Prices vary enormously, so visit as many as possible. You may be able to find a great deal. Always beware of extras, though!

Graphic Artist — in Training

A graphic artist will be able to design beautiful, personalized invitations for you. Unfortunately they will probably cost an arm and a leg, too! Instead, try the art department at a local college. You may be fortunate and find a student willing to take on the project for a far lower cost.

INDIVIDUALIZE YOUR INVITATIONS

Have fun with your invitations. If you are printing them yourself, get together with your family and attendants, and any artistic friends you have, and hold a brainstorming session. Gather all the ideas and try some out.

♥ Wrap the invitation in tissue paper, perhaps with a snowflake pattern if your wedding is in the winter.

♥ Try different colored tissue. Match your wedding colors.

♥ Tie matching — or contrasting — ribbons around the invitation card.

♥ Buy a star shaped stamp — or heart or flower or moon, whatever you particularly like — and print gold or silver patterns.

♥ Press tiny flowers and glue them to the cards.

With a little imagination and a lot of fun, you will be amazed at what you can do. Not only that, but your guests will all be impressed by your handiwork.

All the Extras

You will hear or read over and over again that you *absolutely must* have two envelopes, separate cards for the service and reception, as well as a reply card with its own pre-stamped envelope, in order to avoid a huge etiquette gaff. This is ridiculous. Dig a little deeper and you will find that most of this originates from within the "wedding industry." Of course they want you to spend more! This is not etiquette — it is commercialism!

Try not to be tempted! Put both the service and reception details on one card, together with the reply information and put the card inside one envelope. Most guests will have the good manners to reply in a timely fashion, without the aid of a reply card. Those who don't will benefit from a gentle nudge as you get nearer the day. You will find this to be the case — along with guests who say they are coming but don't show up — whether you supply cards or let guests respond themselves!

At the end of the day, however little or much you spend on your invitations, the chances are only the bride and groom and both sets of parents will keep one. The rest will end up in the trash.

How To Word Your Invitations

In spite of what you may hear to the contrary, there are no rules set in stone as to how you should word your invitations. Look through examples to find what you like the best. Maybe you would prefer to make something up yourself.

Here are some examples of wording, depending upon who will be issuing the invitation. Generally you would use "request the *honour* (spelt this way) of your company" for a religious service and 're-quest the *pleasure* of your company' for a civil ceremony.

Parents of the Bride

Mr and Mrs. John Brown
request the pleasure of your company
at the marriage of their daughter

Elizabeth Jane
and
Mark Philip Black

on Saturday, 20th June, 1997 at 5.00 p.m.
at the Downtown Hotel, Jonesville
immediately followed by a reception

R.S.V.P.
23 Maple Road
Jonesville, NY 12345

Parents of the Bride — Divorced

Mr. James Brown and Mrs. Jane White
request the honour of your company
as they celebrate the marriage of their daughter

Elizabeth Jane
and
Mark Philip Black

on Saturday, 29th December, 1998 at 2.30 p.m.
at The United Methodist Church, Main Street, Sarasota
followed by a reception at the Congress Park

R.S.V.P.
123 Maple Ridge
Sarasota, FL 12345

Both Sets of Parents

Mr. and Mrs. John Brown
and
Mr. and Mrs. Philip Black
invite you to join them as their children

Elizabeth Jane
and
Mark Philip

are united in marriage
on Saturday, August 20th, 1998 at 7.00 p.m.
at 123 Mulberry Avenue, San Francisco
A reception will follow.

R.S.V.P.
123 Mulberry Avenue
San Francisco, CA 12345

Bride and Groom

Miss Elizabeth Jane Brown and Mr. Mark Philip Black
ask you to please join them as they pledge their love
for one another in marriage
on Friday, 7th October, 1998 at 2.00 p.m.
at St. James' Catholic Church, Atlanta

The reception afterwards will be held at
Atlanta Commerce Club, Main Street, Atlanta

R.S.V.P.
123 Westwood Drive
Atlanta, GA 12345

Less Traditional

> Liz and Mark are getting married!
>
> Join us at the top of Willard Mountain
> while we take this momentous step...
> on
> Tuesday, January 3rd, 1998 at 2.00 p.m.
>
> After the service, let's ski down to the
> lodge for food and drinks...
> Call us if you're coming!
> 212-123-4567

Reception Only

It may be impossible to invite everyone you wish to the wedding service itself. If you are inviting guests to the reception only, your invitations might be worded like this:

> Mr. and Mrs. John Brown
> request the pleasure of your company
> at an evening reception to be held at
> La Cave Jazz Club, West Boulevard, Albany
> on Saturday, 14th March, 1998
> to celebrate the marriage of their daughter
>
> Elizabeth Jane
> and
> Mr. Mark Philip Black
>
> R.S.V.P.
> 123 Albany Boulevard,
> Albany, NY 12345

Change who addresses the invitations, depending upon your family situation. Also, as illustrated before, there is absolutely no reason why you cannot make these invitations completely individual and personalized. Go ahead — have fun with these!

CHAPTER SEVEN

· ·

Clothing

And the bride wore . . .

*T*he clothes worn by the bridal party — in particular, the bride — will be one of the most talked about aspects of the wedding. A week from the wedding, few people, if any, will ask what flowers you carried, what the menu was like or how well the band played. But, they will all want to hear about your wedding dress!

When you practiced your mental exercises, to imagine your "dream wedding," what did you see yourself wearing? Was it a sparkling, sequin and jewel bedecked dress or a more simple design? Do you prefer long or short? Must you wear white, ivory or cream?

Your wedding dress is probably going to be the most beautiful dress you will ever wear. For some it is also the most expensive!

This does not have to be the case, though, and there are ways to find the perfect dress for a far more affordable price.

The first thing to do — after you have worked out your clothing budget, that is — is try on some different styles. Take your mom or best friend with you and ask them to be brutally honest. You don't want to pick a dress that looks great from the front but adds six inches to your hips from the rear view! Get an idea of how you look in each style, which will help you choose more easily.

THE BRIDE

Bridal Salons

Although bridal salons seem to have gained a reputation for poor service and overpriced gowns, don't rule them out just yet. If you are set on a traditional style dress which you hope to one day pass down to your daughter, by all means visit the bridal boutiques and check out their sale racks. A bridal store owner, from an extremely reputable store, told me that designer gowns are discounted by up to 50% in January, to make room for the new year's designs.

Take a look at the bridesmaids' dresses, too. You may be surprised. Many of them are available in cream, white or ivory and cost a fraction of the price of a bride's dress.

In general, though, bridal boutiques can be expensive. Staff often work on commission and may try and pressure you to buy a more expensive design. They will also encourage you to buy a larger size, which will then have to be altered to fit. These alterations can run to a couple of hundred dollars!

Discount Bridal Service

The Discount Bridal Service (also known as DBS) is an international "buying service" for brides. They offer discounts of 20% to 40% on almost all nationally advertised wedding dresses. They are able to do this because they don't carry inventory or work out of stores. Instead, they have a nationwide team of representatives who are able to order direct from the manufacturers.

Once you have decided on your wedding dress, all you need to do is call the Discount Bridal Service's National Sales Office at 1-800-874-8794. They will put you in touch with your local representative, who can then take your order. The only disadvantage — and it is a small one — is that orders have to be paid for in full at the time you place them.

Tip: If you found the perfect dress in a bridal salon, look for a picture of it in a bridal magazine and confirm the model number. Some less-than-scrupulous store owners have been known to use their own codes on gowns in order to keep potential customers from doing exactly what I have just suggested you do -- order the same dress at a discounted price! When you call the Discount Bridal Service, let them know which magazine your dress is featured in and on which page. They will then describe the dress to you, so you can be sure you are ordering the one you want. (In defense of bridal salons, I must add that unscrupulous ones are not the norm, and many of them are run by honest, decent sales staff who simply want to earn a living.)

Department or Outlet Stores

What happens to all the unsold prom dresses when the prom season is over? They go on sale! Even before going on sale, prom dresses are considerably less expensive than bridal dresses. Have a look at some of the designs available — they are beautiful.

If you are looking at prom dresses or other evening dresses, why don't you consider something different as far as the color is concerned? Think about the origins of your family. Where did they come from? It may be that in the country of your ancestors, there are age old customs and traditions for you to follow. In some cultures, for example, scarlet is the color for wedding dresses, in others, gold.

White only became the symbol of purity and was adopted as the traditional color for brides, when Queen Victoria, the Queen of England, wore it to marry Prince Albert in 1840. Before that, a bride would be dressed in the best dress she owned, which she would then continue to wear for years to come.

Classified Ads

Check the classified ads in your local paper or even the nearest large city's paper. Weekends are usually the best time. Sadly, not all weddings take place. When a wedding is canceled, the bride is left with a dress, and probably matching veil and other accessories, which she will never wear and cannot take back for a refund. You will see these dresses advertised at a fraction of the price they were bought for.

Although you may feel a little squeamish about turning someone else's misfortune to you advantage, remember, you will be doing her a favor!

You may also see dresses advertised that have been worn. Some brides, having spent a small fortune on their wedding attire, sell it to make a little of their money back.

Thrift and Charity Shops

As in the case of classified ads, some brides will simply take their dress, veil and accessories down to a thrift or charity store. You will be amazed at what you can find at an unbelievably low price.

Some stores will carry a variety of dresses and veils. In fact, I have seen stores that specialize in used bridal clothing, that you can mix and match. You may feel more comfortable trying on a dress in a store, rather than in someone's home.

Rent It

Check your yellow pages for local rental agencies. If you are not concerned about keeping your wedding dress and accessories after the wedding, why not rent them? You could wear a designer gown for a fraction of its value. For local rentals, look up:

- ♥ Bridal Attire
- ♥ Costumes
- ♥ Rentals
- ♥ Wedding Rentals

Make It

This is the option I chose and ended up with my ideal dress — long ivory cotton moiré with a fitted lace bodice — for $35! It only took one weekend, and a girlfriend to keep me company while I sewed, to make it. We still laugh at the shared memory of fitting my ankle length veil, by lying on top of it, on the floor!

The pattern books in sewing stores have dozens of wedding dress designs. Enough to suit every conceivable taste. The design I chose was actually an evening dress. There is also a huge selection of fabrics available. Some stores specialize in bridal fabrics — the ones I visited didn't seem to charge any more than regular fabric stores, either.

Of course not everyone can sew — or enjoys sewing. If this sounds like you, ask around among your family and close friends. The chances are you will find at least one talented seamstress, who would be only too delighted — not to mention flattered — to help out.

Are there any design colleges near you? Or a community college with a strong art or design department? You may be able to find a talented but penniless student, who will be delighted by the opportunity to earn a little by making your dress.

♥ .... ♥

Tip: If someone is making the dress for you, take them with you to choose the pattern, fabric, etc. They know what their capabilities are and whether they can make something or not. Don't try to pressure them into making something they are not confident enough to do.

♥ .... ♥

If you draw a blank looking for a friend, relative or student who sews, try a professional. Shop around, listen to recommendations and ask to see some of their work.

You will probably find the quality of their work far superior to anything coming from a bridal manufacturer — and be pleasantly surprised by their prices.

Borrow It

Is there an heirloom gown in your family? What did your mother or grandmother wear at their weddings? Can it be altered to fit you? Maybe you have a sister whose dress you could wear?

Not only would you look wonderful, but imagine how your mother would feel, watching you exchange your wedding vows in the very same dress she wore! Perhaps one day you may watch your own daughter wear it, too. What beautiful memories that dress would carry with it!

Headdresses and Veils

Once you have chosen your dress, it is time to decide what to wear as a headdress. As with the dress, what you wear on our head will be influenced, in part, by your choice of where to hold the wedding. For example, a hat may be more suitable for an outside wedding — if only to help shade your eyes from the sun.

Consider the climate where you live, too. If it is hot and humid, you may want to avoid fresh flowers for an outdoor wedding. At least be careful in your choice, some can wilt incredibly quickly!

You may have been fortunate enough to find a veil in a thrift or charity shop or perhaps you are able to borrow an heirloom veil. If not, why not make one? You don't need to be a great seamstress to make your own veil. Even the most artistically challenged among us will find it simple. Craft and sewing stores now sell everything you need, ready for assembly. For around $20 you can buy the veil, cut to size and already seamed. All you need to do is choose the length you want and attach it to a comb or headband! You will not need anything more than a needle and thread — and talent is not required!

Making your Veil from Scratch

1. Decide on the length you want your veil to be and how many layers you would like.
2. Calculate the amount of tulle or lace you will need. This can be bought at fabric stores, with prices starting at less than one dollar per yard!
3. Cut the tulle into the appropriate lengths. If you are having a two layer veil, don't worry about cutting, just fold it.

4. Hem the tulle all round. Using your sewing machine on the zigzag setting, stitch around the entire piece, or pieces, of fabric.
5. Gather the tulle together at the top. Depending on what you are attaching the veil to — a comb, headband or clip — pull the gathers to the correct width and stitch tightly.
6. Attach the tulle to your comb, headband or clip either by sewing or using plastic covered wire.

You can decorate the headdress as you like. For example, if you are wearing a beaded dress, use fabric glue to glue beads onto a headband.

If you prefer fresh flowers, attach the veil to a comb and, on your wedding day, use some plastic covered wire (green gardening wire works well) to attach the flowers. It is extremely simple to make and the effect is lovely.

Underwear and Footwear

It is important to choose your underwear and shoes early. If you are making your dress, or having one altered or made for you, wear the bra you have chosen to any fittings. This will ensure that the dress fits in all the right places. Also, wear your shoes for a correct hem length.

The most important thing to bear in mind, though, is that you will be wearing your wedding outfit for several hours — make sure that your shoes and underwear are comfortable! It's amazing how much sore, pinched feet or creeping underwear can spoil your pleasure!

If possible, try to avoid fabric shoes. They are not very flexible when your feet start to swell — which they are guaranteed to do during your wedding, especially if you and your new hubby plan to dance the night away.

♥ . . . . ♥

Tip: Whatever shoes you choose, buy them towards the end of the day, when your feet will be swollen, pretty much as they will at your wedding. Try to wear them around the house as much as possible before the wedding. This will help avoid blisters.

♥ . . . . ♥

THE BRIDE'S ATTENDANTS

Bridesmaids and Maid/Matron of Honor

Be kind to your attendants! So says a former bridesmaid who is still trying to live down a turquoise polyester shepherdess dress! Choose a style, color and fabric that will not only suit them but that they can wear again. It is pretty much accepted now that the bridesmaids buy their own dresses. They may be on a tight budget too, so take that into consideration.

All the same rules used when buying the bride's dress apply for the attendants, too. You always have the options to buy, rent, borrow or make their dresses.

If your wedding will be small and intimate, consider having just one attendant. It is much easier to find one dress that you like, either on sale in a bridal store, department store or in a thrift or charity shop. If you prefer to have several attendants, you may find this hard to do.

Remember, though, that the bridesmaids or matron of honor may be able to make their own dresses or have someone in their families who can help.

Making the Bridesmaid's Dresses

If you are having more than one attendant, take them all to the fabric store with you at the same time. When you have all agreed on the design of the dress and found the perfect fabric for it, *buy all the fabric at the same time.* This is essential, as dye lots in fabric can vary dramatically from batch to batch. If you don't buy all the fabric from the same dye lot, you may end up with different color dresses.

Younger Attendants

There are few sights quite as charming as little flower girls scattering petals or a young ring bearer proudly walking up the aisle with his precious pillow! If you have young relatives or friends with children, you may choose to include them in your wedding. A word of warning, though, there are never any guarantees that the children will want to 'perform' on the day! You will find it a much more relaxing and enjoyable experience if you just let the children look cute and don't expect too much from them. The pressure can be frightening for them.

Flowergirls

It is easy to go a little overboard with clothes for the small attendants. Instead, why not go for something practical? Parents will appreciate an outfit that their children can wear again.

♥ Try a cotton smock, that matches your dress, with a contrasting sash in the color the bridesmaids are wearing.

♥ If you don't want to make a dress, try department store party dresses. They look delightful and can be used several times over.

♥ Look for party dresses at Easter. They come in pastel shades that are perfect for a wedding. After Easter they go on sale!

♥ Inside or outside, if you have a soft surface to walk on, such as carpet or lawn, let the flower girl go barefoot. Not only will you save on the price of shoes and tights, but young children love to go barefoot!

♥ Buy a flower basket at a craft store for next to nothing. Put an oasis inside and fill it with greenery. Add a few randomly placed flowers to match your bouquet. For extra effect, tie ribbons from the basket's handle and let them hang freely.

♥ If you prefer not to arrange flowers, put a small potted flowering plant in the basket.

♥ If your flower girl will be scattering petals, use a craft store basket with ribbons and fill it with potpourri or loose petals.

♥ In spite of the name, flower girls don't have to carry flowers. Use you imagination. They could carry song books or bibles, which they could then keep as your gift to them.

Ring Bearer

The ring bearer is generally a little boy (although I have seen the role more than adequately performed by a dog!). Again, it is easy to get carried away dressing him. Try some of these suggestions instead.

♥ Instead of hiring a miniature tuxedo, try a pair of linen shorts. They could be black, gray, white or the color the bridesmaids are wearing. A white shirt and bow tie will finish the outfit off beautifully.

♥ If the wedding is a more casual outdoor affair, skip the shirt and bow tie and go for a polo shirt instead.

♥ If you don't find a ring pillow that appeals to you, leave it out. Have the ring bearer carry the rings in his pocket or on an open bible.

♥ Make the pillow instead of buying it. All you need to do is cover a small cushion in a fabric to match your dress. Sew two squares together — no one will be close enough to inspect the quality of the stitching!

THE GROOM

Although the poor groom seems to take a back seat to the bride at weddings, a young man, or older man for that matter, always looks wonderful dressed in his best suit or a tuxedo.

Although there are fewer options available for the groom, for example, it would take a professional to make a suit, there are still areas in which you can watch the cost.

Depending upon the style of your wedding, the groom can choose between a suit, a tuxedo or tails. If he is in the military, he may prefer to wear his uniform. If the wedding is outdoors, a smart suit would be most suitable, or, for an evening wedding, a tuxedo. Tails should be reserved for formal church weddings.

Does your fiancé have a suit that you would love him to wear? Maybe he and his attendants could wear ties to match the color you have chosen for your bridesmaids.

Some tuxedo rental firms will offer special deals. If you are using, for example, a photographer who is affiliated with the tuxedo rental store, you may be offered discounts. Sometimes, if enough groomsmen are renting, the groom's tuxedo will be offered free of charge. Encourage your fiancé to shop around and find out all the options before committing himself.

Groomsmen and Best Man

The groomsmen and best man should be dressed the same as the groom. The exception to this would be if the groom is in the armed forces and the groomsmen and best man are not, in which case they would wear whatever the groom chooses for them.

Military Weddings

If either the bride or groom is in the armed forces, they are entitled to wear their uniform at their wedding. Any dress uniform looks spectacular at a wedding. The only word of caution, however, is that you should check the rules for the wedding location before wearing a saber. Some churches, for example, consider them weapons and will not allow them on the premises.

CHAPTER EIGHT

. . . .

 # *Flowers & Decorations*

Deck the halls

*F*lowers can take up a major part of your wedding budget if you are not careful. A package deal at a florist, in a larger metropolitan area, could set you back several thousand dollars!

Ask yourself if you really need all those flowers? Is there something else you could use instead? There are certainly enough options available to help any bride, no matter what her budget is.

Using the following checklist, decide which flowers you absolutely cannot do without. Anything else, leave out or substitute.

- ❁ Bridal bouquet
- ❁ Bridal headpiece
- ❁ Bride's attendants' bouquets

- Bride's attendants' headpieces
- Flower girls
- Corsages for the mothers and grandmothers of the bride and groom
- Boutonnières for the groom
- Boutonnières for the best man and groomsmen
- Boutonnières for the fathers and grandfathers of the bride and groom
- Flower arrangement for the alter
- Pew end arrangements
- Table centerpieces for the reception

You can see how the costs mount up, if you choose everything!

The Language of Flowers

Throughout history, it has been believed that certain flowers and herbs hold different meanings. If you follow superstitions, you may wish to consider this when choosing your flowers.

- Chrysanthemums — *truth*
- Clover — *good luck*
- Daisies — *gentleness*
- Fern — *fascination*
- Forget-me-nots — *true love*
- Ivy — *fidelity*
- Roses, red — *everlasting love*
- Roses, white — *innocent love*
- Roses, yellow — *devotion and friendship*
- Roses, red and white together — *unity*

Because herbs were believed to ward off evil, brides from years ago carried fragrant nosegays of lavender, rosemary and thyme. Why not include some in your bouquet?

What's in Season

Although it is now possible to import pretty much any flower at any time of year, the costs can become astronomical. Selecting flowers that are in season will instantly bring the price down. Check with your local flower market for availability.

- ❀ Spring — tulips, daffodils
- ❀ Summer — roses
- ❀ Fall — wildflowers
- ❀ Winter — carnations

Freeze Dried or Silk Flowers

Keep in mind that fresh flowers are not your only option. Freeze dried flowers will look exactly like fresh flowers, but can last for years. After the wedding, you could use your bouquet as a table centerpiece or wall hanging in your new home! Over the years, silk flowers have become more realistic to look at, too.

If your wedding is at a time of year when the flowers of your choice are out of season, you could have your bouquet made, or make it yourself, months in advance.

An added benefit to making your own bouquet, of course, is that you can see how it looks before the wedding and you will have time to make any changes you want. This would also apply to any other flower arrangements you have chosen.

The Bridal Bouquet

Of all the flowers you decide you *must* have, the bridal bouquet is probably top of your list! Very few brides decide to go without. When choosing the style of your bouquet, consider some of these points:

⊛ The bridal bouquet should blend in and complement the bride's dress, not overshadow it. If you dress is simple, your flowers must be, too. Similarly, if you are wearing a more ornate gown, you should carry a more ornate bouquet.

⊛ Balance the size of the bouquet. A small nosegay would look completely swamped if your dress has a full skirt and train. A fuller dress calls for a fuller bouquet.

Although anything goes as far as the style of your bouquet is concerned, four styles have remained consistently popular: Posy, Cascade, Simple Ann Bouquet and Single Stem Flower.

Using a Professional Florist

If you have budgeted for a professionally made bouquet, visit several florists in your area before you decide on one. Some will only make the standard bouquets shown in bridal flower books, others will custom make your bouquet. Depending upon the style you have chosen, the time of year and what flowers are in season, you can have a custom made wedding bouquet for as little as $30.

Develop a relationship with your florist — this will make her job much easier. It is also helpful to put together a checklist of what you are looking for before you visit her. I recommend taking pictures of the following with you:

* Any bouquets that you particularly like
* Your favorite flowers — especially if you are unsure of the flower's name
* Your dress
* Where you are holding the ceremony

Check that the florist uses only the freshest blooms and greenery, as this will ensure a longer lasting bouquet. Be sure to ask her advice about care of the flowers.

If you decide to have any of the other flowers made by a professional, take along pictures that will help. Be sure to give her the contact name, telephone number and address of a site coordinator, where you are holding your ceremony or reception; she will need to arrange a delivery time. You will also need to give the address and telephone number of where you want the bouquet to be delivered, if it differs from the address on your order. If you are getting ready at a hotel or a relative's house, check these details first. You don't want your flowers going to the wrong place!

Remember, delivery is extra, so pick the flowers up if you can!

Making a Bouquet

Making your own bouquet is not as difficult as it looks. Everything you need is readily available at any craft store, along with easy to follow guides to making any conceivable style of flower arrangement. If you have never listed flower arranging as one of your talents (I haven't!), you may want to practice first, especially if you have selected a more ornate bouquet.

Try to go for impact — make the whole bouquet out of one particular flower. If you choose a heavily fragrant flower, such as vibernum, sweet peas or roses, you will have the added pleasure of a beautiful scent. Include a lot of greenery, if possible, such as ivy and fern. It bulks out the bouquet and costs very little — especially if you can pick it yourself!

Check your local community college or high school for night classes. Invest in a course of flower arranging lessons, which you can put to use throughout your life!

Still not confident? Ask some of the students at the night classes to make the bouquet for you! Florists have to learn their trade somewhere, before they become professionals.

Bouquet Toss

Whether you make your own bouquet, or have a friend or professional make it, decide before the wedding whether you want to sacrifice it in the bouquet toss, or not. If you plan to preserve your bouquet as a precious keepsake, hang on to it!

When the time comes to toss your bouquet, use a throwaway bunch of flowers instead. You don't need more than a couple of flowers, preferably matching your bouquet, tied with ribbon. This is becoming increasingly accepted and no one minds — especially the girl who catches them!

Preserving your Bouquet

There are more options than simply pressing or hanging flowers now! Try some of these:

- Freeze dry and make it into a wreath or table centerpiece.
- Make the petals into potpourri.
- Use something with a root attached, such as ivy, and plant it in your garden.

Flowers for the Bride's Attendants
And Bridal Party

The flowers your attendants carry do not need to be ornate at all. Their dresses will generally be simpler designs than the bride's, and should, as such, be complemented by simpler flowers. You may even decide to have them carry something other than a bouquet. Popular variations are:

- ❀ Single rose, or other flower, tied with ribbon
- ❀ Bible or hymn book
- ❀ Candlestick with lit candle — use the non-drip variety!
- ❀ Dish of potpourri
- ❀ Velvet or faux fur muff or gloves

Use your imagination! Have you seen any bridesmaids who carried something unusual that caught your attention?

Flowergirls

Flowergirls look adorable — even when they don't carry flowers! Collect rose petals from your garden or a nearby park to fill their baskets. Perhaps they could carry a dish of bon-bons, or a smaller version of the single flower your bridesmaids are carrying.

Headpieces

If you or any of your attendants are wearing fresh flower headpieces, unless you want a full crown of flowers, buy or make a corsage and attach it to a plastic comb with twist wire. Having just one corsage professionally made can be very reasonably priced and, with or without a veil, looks beautiful.

Are your attendants wearing their hair up? For an effective, natural look, tuck a couple of loose flowers into the back of their hair.

Corsages and Boutonnières

The price can really start mounting, if you have the corsages and boutonnieres made. Over the years they have become increasingly ornate, when really they need not be.

For the gentlemen — the groom, groomsmen, fathers and grandfathers of the bride and groom — a single flower head, such as a rose or carnation, is perfectly sufficient and looks wonderful! Or, why not go for something out of the ordinary, such as a daisy, sunflower or lily?

To make them, buy a bunch of the flowers you have chosen (supermarkets or flower markets are usually the cheapest source) and cut the stems about two inches from the flower. If you want to dress it up a little, put a small piece of greenery behind the flower and tie them with a piece of ribbon that matches the bride's dress. Supply a regular dressmaking pin so that they can be pinned to lapels. You could make enough for everyone for less that it costs to have one identical boutonnière professionally made!

The mothers and grandmothers of the bride and groom will have taken great care with what they wear to the wedding — do they really want to have half their dresses covered by a flower arrangement? Make their corsages the same way as the boutonnières, but use two or three flowers and a larger ribbon.

Where to Find Your Flowers

There are many more places than a florist shop to find flowers.

- Flower markets — where do the florists buy their flowers?
- Farmers markets
- Supermarkets
- Your own back yard
- Mother nature's garden — the countryside
- Local gardening clubs
- Friends and neighbors

Decorating the Ceremony Site

Think about the setting in which you are holding your marriage ceremony. Is it a church or an outdoor site, for example. This will help you to decide how little or how much you need to add in the way of flowers or decorations.

Church

How old is your church? If it is a historical building, you may not need to add anything at all. Old churches have their own atmosphere and beauty that it is almost a shame to detract from. If your church is newer, however, it may look a little bare. The addition of some wedding decor can make it more festive.

There are numerous ways to decorate a church using few, if any, flowers.

1. **_Tulle_** — this low cost netted fabric is wonderful for decorating. It needs no hemming or sewing and is stiff enough to fashion into large bows. It can also withstand beads being glued to it, using fabric glue, and looks wonderful bunched up and tied with ribbon. Best use: pew ends.
2. **_Candles_** — their warm glow softens any atmosphere. Best use: the altar.
3. **_Greenery_** — cut branches with blossom on or decorate with ribbons. Best use: over doors and arches.
4. **_Bunches of Herbs_** — tie bunches of mixed herbs with ribbons. Best use: pew ends.

Keep in mind that at certain times of the year churches will be decorated already. At Christmas, for example, what more would you want to add than a couple of candles?

Have you seen your church dressed up for a harvest festival? You can copy this at other times of the year, too. Decorate it with baskets of fruit which can later be used in your reception or handed out to needy families. A couple of potted plants and some tulle swathed around can make a spectacular — and reusable — altar piece.

Hotel

Any of the suggestions given for decorating a church can be adapted to suit a hotel. If your ceremony is inside, use tulle, greenery and ribbons to decorate the sides of the chairs that form the aisle. A few flowers or bunches of herbs can be added for extra effect.

Ask about renting plants. You can line the aisle with variegated leaf plants, decorated with tulle and ribbons in your wedding colors. For a festive air, tie balloons to the backs of seats.

For Jewish couples using a chuppah, decorate it with tulle and greenery, or a light, gauzy fabric, before adding a bare minimum of flowers. After all, it is intended to symbolize the nomadic tents of Israel — which I am sure were not nearly as ornate as some of the chuppahs used in weddings today!

Outside Venue

Mother Nature can be a pretty hard act to beat. So why try? Accentuate a few areas, particularly the "altar," but other than that, leave well enough alone!

Use flowering potted plants, borrowed, rented or bought, as much as possible, if you want to add color. Find some pots and paint your names and the date, and maybe even a message of thanks, on them. After the wedding, you can give one to everyone who helped with your wedding. They make wonderful "thank you" gifts.

If your outside venue leaves a little to be desired, as far as decor is concerned, again, use potted plants as much as possible. If your wedding is taking place somewhere such as a rooftop, you can use a screen with tulle and greenery to cover large areas such as pipes and ducts. If you cannot find a screen, a low cost alternative is to buy three plant trellises and attach them at the top, middle and bottom. Zigzag them so that they stand up securely. Because most of them will already be white or green, they are guaranteed to match at least some of your wedding colors!

Whatever location you have chosen, though, there will be at least one special reason why you chose it — whether it is a beautiful old church, a garden, or a rooftop with a view of the city. And, don't forget that on your wedding day, all eyes will be on the bride and groom — not the flowers!

DECORATING FOR
THE RECEPTION

Unless there is something that you really want to cover up or disguise, there is very little you need to do to decorate your reception site. Aside from a few table centerpieces, hotels, restaurants and bars will need little to no decorations. The same holds true if you are hosting your reception in your home or garden; it only takes a little imagination to achieve delightful results.

You can have a lot of fun with table decorations! A small investment of time can save a lot of money. Following are some ideas that have been successfully used by other brides:

Bunches of flowers in small vases — they don't have to match. In fact, it can look very striking if you use a different vase and flowers on each table.

Floating candles — put a couple of floating candles (check you supermarket for packs of six) in a clear glass bowl, along with one or two fresh flower heads. If the bowl is larger and you prefer to use more flowers, choose something like a chrysanthemum — you can buy a plant for a couple of dollars and cut numerous flowers from it.

Standing candles — buy candles in your wedding colors, tie a ribbon around them and slip a single flower or some herbs inside the ribbon. Alternatively, use white candles, tied with ribbons in your wedding colors. Keep the ribbons long and let them cascade down to the table.

Potted plants — paint designs on the pots. Mark them with your names and the date, they will make a great souvenir! Alternatively, wrap the pots in tulle and tie with them ribbons.

Dishes of pot pourri — add a beautiful scent as well as color.

Reception program — especially if you have a time restriction. Print a card showing the times that food will be served, bar times, and when the dancing will start. If you have a time restriction, show what time the reception will end. An old fashioned, but quaint, way to do this is to mark "Carriages at (time)," at the bottom of the card.

Favors

If you are giving out favors (and please don't feel that you have to), why not incorporate them into your table decorations? Make your favors and place them in a dish in the center of each table. Or lay them above each place setting. Here are some suggestions:

♥ The most familiar favor is the bag of three Jordan almonds, said to symbolize the bitter-sweet nature of marriage, wrapped in lace or net.

♥ Miniature heart-shaped soaps, in you wedding colors. For extra effect, wrap them in tulle. If the soaps are scented, you will have the added benefit of their lovely smell.

♥ Miniature flower shaped floating candles. Instead of lighting them, wrap them and place them in a dish. As with the soaps, they are often scented.

♥ Book marks. Make book marks for each of your guests. You could write a much loved poem on them or simply a message such as "Thank you for sharing our special day," with your names and the date below.

♥ If you are holding a Christmas wedding, buy bags of ornaments and a gold glitter pen. Write your names and the date on the ornaments. You can then thread them with a little ribbon and use them as napkin rings.

♥ Bake heart-shaped cookies (you can buy them in a pack if you prefer). Using a frosting tube, write your names on top.

As you can see, a little imagination and effort can make your flower and decoration budget go a long way. And who would ever be able to tell?

. . . .

CHAPTER NINE

Photographs & Video

Lights, camera, action!

*Y*our wedding will rush by in such a blur, you will be grateful to have it beautifully recorded on film, either in still photographs, a video or both. There is something incredibly exciting about putting your album together, rewatching the video and talking over all the high points of the wedding. For years to come, you will be able to enjoy looking back on your special day.

Professional vs. Amateur Photographer

Choosing the right person to record these precious memories can be a difficult task. Photographing a wedding is a challenge. On top of it being an emotion-packed day, the photographer has only one chance to capture the event. Before choosing a photographer, consider their qualifications very carefully.

Professional Photographer

Although there is no doubt that a well-qualified, experienced wedding photographer *should* do the best job, their package prices can cost thousands of dollars. And, the chances are, if you are reading this book, this simply does not fit into your budget. In fact, it may well be your entire budget!

If going with a professional is an absolute *must have* for you, be sure to follow these suggestions:

- Shop around — gather quotes from several studios. Who knows, they may even try to undercut each other's prices!

- Ask around — word of mouth is always the best reference. You can tell very little from an advertisement.

- Look at examples of their work — ask to see at least one completed album from a recent wedding, taken by the actual person who will be photographing yours.

- Meet with the person who will be taking your pictures — do you get along with him? If you feel uncomfortable in any way, don't book him! It is essential that you bond well with the photographer as this will come over in the pictures. Besides, you certainly don't want someone ordering you and your guests around all day!

- Check how long you will have the photographer for — if you go over their time limit, you may find you are charged extra.

- Read the small print in the contract — you don't want to find any extra charges after the wedding!

♥ *Tip: Ask to see the entire set of proofs from a previous wedding the photographer has done — these will be unedited. This way you will have a better idea of how well the photographer takes pictures. There will always be some proofs that cannot be used — someone always blinks — but how many of the proofs are unusable because they are just not good pictures?* ♥

What to look for in your Photographer

As I mentioned earlier, it is essential that you feel at ease with your photographer. You don't want to feel stiff and uncomfortable in the pictures — it will show!

Many photographers work with different styles. Look at photos they have take and see if they fit in with your ideas. Do the pictures look too formally posed? Do you prefer something a little more relaxed? Will the photographer go along with your wishes? Will he or she let you pose a certain way? Are they patient enough to work with small children as well as over-emotional adults? How do they compensate for bad lighting conditions or weather that won't oblige?

What to look for in the Contract

Never sign a contract until you have read it thoroughly and had time to fully understand everything it includes! Look out for these points:

- *Who will be taking the pictures?* Make sure you have met with them, liked them and their work. Make sure their name is specified in the contract. You don't want to find a different photographer turning up on the day. Ask what happens if the photographer cannot make it on the day.

• **What time will the photographer arrive?** How much time do you have? Does this include travel time? You don't want to find that you have paid for a package lasting five hours, when in reality, two hours are taken up in travel, with the photographer arriving at the site an hour before you. Equally, you don't want to find extra travel charges added to your bill.

• **What exactly will be included in your package?** And I mean exactly! Check for all the hidden extras and ask for them to be listed clearly in the contract.

Of course you will also need to confirm payment terms and the date when your proofs and pictures will be ready.

Using Freelance and Amateur Photographers

There are several ways to find a professional photographer without paying the full price, if you are prepared to put a little more effort into the search! Try some of these options.

Freelance Photographers

Look in your local newspapers. Many of the photographs used are supplied by freelancers. Because few papers pay well for the pictures, the photographers may welcome the opportunity for some additional income. Call the paper and leave a message for them or ask for a number where you can reach them.

Photographic Stores

Many of the staff in photographic stores are skilled photographers — and have access to the most up-to-date equipment! Call into any photo supply store and ask. If they cannot help you themselves, you can bet that they know of someone who can!

Art College or Adult Education

If you have an art college locally, call to ask about their photography classes. They may have an instructor who can take your pictures, or a talented student, who charges even less.

If you don't have a college dedicated to arts nearby, try the art department at any local college. Don't rule out adult education classes, either. If you can find a local photography class, the tutor, or a student, may also be available to take wonderful pictures.

Using Friends and Family as Photographers

Although any other book on wedding planning is likely to tell you that picking an amateur photographer is the worst thing you can possibly do, this is not always the case! Almost all of the brides I interviewed for this book opted for an amateur photographer to take their wedding pictures. Without exception, they were completely delighted with the results. In fact, I am the only one who had any problems! Even though things did go wrong with my pictures, they were corrected for very little cost (I will cover this topic a little later).

If, like mine, your budget is really small, hiring a professional photographer is out of the question. Using a talented amateur is your only choice. By following the tips listed below, you can ensure the best possible pictures for the lowest possible price:

- *If possible, ask more than one responsible person to take the pictures.* Make sure they are up to the task and don't have a tendency to cut heads off! Arrange for one person to specifically cover the service, and another the reception, with a couple of candid pictures to be taken in between.
- *Supply plenty of rolls of film — and always make sure you have a few spares.* If you don't use them up at the wedding, take them on your honeymoon!

- **Check the batteries in the cameras being used!** This is especially important if you need to use the flash.
- **When using a flash, try to avoid "red-eye."** You can do this by turning slightly to the side for pictures instead of looking straight into the lens. Alternatively, there are cameras on the market now, that cut the problem out all together — use one if you can, for all flash pictures.
- **Use a good camera.** If the person taking the pictures does not have a reliable camera, borrow or hire one.
- **Make sure pictures may be taken during the ceremony.** Talk to the officiant before the service. If pictures are not allowed during the wedding ceremony, arrange to pose for pictures after the service.
- **Try to avoid posing in straight lines.** You don't want your wedding pictures to look like a line up at a police station! Opt for more natural groupings. Check through friends' or relatives' wedding albums for groupings and poses that you particularly like.
- **Take candid as well as posed shots.** These will reflect the tone of the day far more realistically.
- **Watch the background.** Try to avoid a background that is too busy. Be careful of statues or wildlife. You don't want the groom to look as if he has an extra arm or set of horns!
- **Look around for picture perfect settings.** Visit the site before the wedding and pose for some pictures. Get them developed before the wedding, to see which settings look the best. Try to do this at the same time of day as the wedding — this will help give an idea of the lighting.
- **Avoid looking into the sun.** You don't want everyone in the picture squinting! Also, avoid standing with the sun directly behind you or in too much shadow.

Advantages of Using an Amateur

  ☝ If a friend is taking your pictures, you will already know them well and will feel much more at ease while the pictures are being taken.

  ☝ There is no limit on the time they can spend taking the photographs or the number of pictures that can be taken.

  ☝ You will only have to pay for film and developing.

  ☝ The negatives are yours to reprint as often as you need; you will be amazed how many times you will need to do this!

Disadvantages of Using an Amateur

  ☞ The pressure of taking your once-in-a-lifetime pictures may be too much for a friend. A normally good photographer may make mistakes because of nerves. Ease the pressure by asking more than one person to take pictures. Let them know that they will not be alone.

  ☞ Their equipment is generally not as sophisticated as a professional would use. This may cause problems if lighting conditions are poor. Try some pictures in advance. Take them at the same time of day and see how the light is. If it is bad, choose somewhere else for your pictures or rent the appropriate equipment.

When Things Go Wrong

Yes, things can go wrong, whether you hire a professional wedding photographer or ask a friend to help. Fortunately, there are sophisticated machines that can correct most mistakes.

I speak from personal experience! This happened at my wedding. A friend of my husband's had trained in a professional photographic studio and offered to take our wedding pictures as his gift.

He still had all the equipment — fancy camera, light meters, etc. — and we had seen plenty of his work, which was very impressive. On our wedding day, though, a combination of champagne, nerves and his ex-girlfriend showing up, got the better of him, and he set the camera's shutter speed incorrectly!

When we picked up the prints, we were devastated to find that half the frame was overexposed and half underexposed. I, of course, burst into tears right there in the store! When I finally calmed down, I called some studios to see if anything could be done to salvage any of the pictures. With the aid of computers, one studio was able to help us. For very little cost, too! We now have a beautiful album of photographs.

Funny enough though, our favorite pictures of the wedding, the ones that captured us most closely, and are the ones we display proudly in our home, are all casual shots taken by guests!

Don't let our experience put you off — it could happen to either a professional or an amateur. Just remember, before you go into a state of hysteria, if and when things do go wrong, there are ways to put them right.

Formal Wedding Portrait

Many people choose to have their formal wedding portraits taken sometime other than on their wedding day. The greatest benefit of this is that your hair will be perfect and all the emotion won't have done a number on your make up!

You could select a private studio for the portraits or choose one of the photographers in a department store. The department store will generally be much cheaper and you can view several pictures before selecting the one you want.

If you and the groom are having a picture taken together, consider having it taken before the wedding. The tradition of not seeing the bride in her finery before the wedding, dates back to the days when all marriages were arranged — when either the bride or groom may have called it off, if they were disappointed by the looks of their future spouse! This is unlikely to happen to you! If you prefer to keep with the tradition, though, arrange to have the pictures taken before any clothing you have hired has to be returned.

PHOTOGRAPH CHECKLIST

Decide ahead of time what pictures you would like taken. Write down who will be in each photograph and discuss the list with the photographer. This way you will ensure that no one gets left out, no feelings are hurt and you get all the pictures you want! The following is a checklist for you to use, to make sure that no photo opportunities are missed during any stage of your big day.

Before the Service:

❑ Bride in dress
❑ Bride with her mother
❑ Bride with her father
❑ Bride with both parents or parent and appropriate stepparent
❑ Bride with honor attendant
❑ Bride with all attendants
❑ Bride with flowers
❑ Bride leaving the house (or wherever she is getting ready)
❑ Bride in the car
❑ Groom alone
❑ Groom looking pensive at wedding site, awaiting the arrival of his bride
❑ Groom with his best man
❑ Groom with all his attendants

The Ceremony:

❑ Bride with her father, getting out of car
❑ Bride with her father, arriving at the ceremony site
❑ Maid of Honor attending to the bride's veil
❑ Ushers escorting guests
❑ Arrival of the groom's parents
❑ Groom and groomsmen at the alter
❑ Bridesmaids walking up the aisle
❑ Matron of honor, walking up the aisle
❑ Flowergirl and ringbearer walking up the aisle
❑ Bride with her father, walking up the aisle
❑ Bride's father giving her away
❑ Groom meeting his bride
❑ Bride and groom at the alter
❑ Bride and groom exchanging vows
❑ Bride and groom exchanging rings
❑ The Kiss!
❑ Bride and groom walking down the aisle
❑ Bride and groom outside
❑ Bride and groom with the wedding party
❑ Bride and groom with their parents
❑ Bride and groom in the car

Before the Reception:

❑ Bride's attendants admiring her ring
❑ Close up of the bride's and groom's hands, showing rings
❑ Bride and groom together
❑ Bride with her parents
❑ Groom with his parents
❑ Bride and groom with maid of honor and best man
❑ Bride with all the attendants

- ❑ Groom with all the attendants
- ❑ Bride and groom with all the wedding party
- ❑ Bride and groom with both sets of parents

The Reception:

- ❑ Bride and groom arriving
- ❑ Bride and groom at table
- ❑ Bride and groom dancing
- ❑ Bride and her father dancing
- ❑ Groom and his mother dancing
- ❑ The cake
- ❑ Cutting the cake
- ❑ Bride and groom feeding each other cake
- ❑ The toasts
- ❑ Bride throwing her bouquet
- ❑ Bride and groom, ready to leave

During the reception, you may also choose to leave disposable cameras on each table. Encourage one responsible person from each table to take pictures and return the camera to you afterwards. This way you will end up capturing some terrific moments that may otherwise have been missed.

Black and White Photos vs. Color

This is really a matter of personal taste. Black and white photographs can look very classical and may be a little lower in cost. However, if you

want to catch more realism, opt for color. You may also wish to consider a combination of the two — black and white for the formal pictures, and color for the more candid shots.

Accessories

Wedding albums come in all shapes, sizes and qualities. They also come in a wide variety of prices. And they make perfect wedding gifts! If you prefer to choose our own, though, why not consider a plain white leather bound album? If you are making your wedding dress, try to keep enough left over fabric to cover an album! You may choose to keep more than one album, too. It is a lovely idea to have one containing your more formal wedding pictures, another showing the candid photos and a third chronicling the time that you and your fiancé have been together, from your first date to the wedding. This could include pictures taken while preparing for the wedding — sampling foods, trying on your dress, a momento from the night he proposed!

If you decide to use a professional photographer, many of them will include an album in their wedding package. If you are not happy with their choice, ask to be discounted by the amount it costs. Many photographers will also offer, and encourage, albums of pictures as gifts for both sets of parents and the attendants. Beware! These extras can become very expensive.

VIDEO

You will miss so much of what is going on throughout your wedding day, that capturing it on video is a wonderful way to catch up with it all afterwards. You will be able to hear everyone's comments and conversation, along with the visual recording.

Professional Video

A professional video can be a beautifully produced package, with titles, stills, music, and even footage of you and your fiancé as children. It can also cost more than buying a video camera yourselves!

When you begin looking for a professional videographer, follow pretty much the same tips as you would when looking for a photographer. You need to establish a rapport with the person taking the video.

- This is your wedding day, not a staged media event, so try to keep the camera as unobtrusive as possible.
- How long will the videographer spend at the service and reception? How long will the final tape be?
- What exactly is included in their package?
- Are there overtime charges or any hidden extras?
- Will the videographer observe your wishes?
- Will he or she include interviews with guests?

Be sure not to miss out on these special "interviews." List ahead of time anyone you would like the videographer to capture on tape. Remember to include older relatives, such as grandparents, as well as parents and close friends. You could even have a mix of some rehearsed comments and some spontaneous.

Amateur Videographer

Having a friend or relative take the video can be more relaxed and natural. Just make sure that they really know how to work the camera! Ask them to practice with the camera they are using and try to visit the wedding site for a rehearsal.

One of the most common mistakes made by amateur videographers is to move the camera too quickly, while trying to capture everything. The end result of this will be motion sickness for anyone watching the film! To avoid any problems such as this, follow these suggestions:

- Use a tripod to avoid a wobbling picture.
- Use new film.
- Check that the camera's batteries are fully charged. Carry back-ups — some batteries don't last long!
- Check in advance that all the equipment is working properly.
- Discuss with the videographer, before the wedding, exactly what you would like included. For example, guests arriving at the church, the entire service, interviews with best friends, parents, grandparents, etc.
- Share the job! Have more than one person take a turn behind the camera. As with the still photographs, this will take the pressure off.

. . . .

$\mathcal{T}$ransportation

Get me to the church on time!

$\mathcal{D}$epending upon where you hold your service and reception, transportation may need to be arranged. If you are not as fortunate as some brides are, who are able to walk to their weddings, consider all your choices before spending a huge amount of money hiring a car.

Limousines

Unless you have a friend or relative who happens to own a limousine, rental can become extremely expensive. If you don't have a limo ride to church at the top of your fantasy list — forget it!

Luxury Car

For a fraction of the cost of a limousine, you can rent a luxury or convertible car for the full day. Decorated with ribbons on the hood and each door handle, a rental car can be a reasonably priced and spectacular option.

A smartly dressed chauffeur would perfect the image. Ask a reliable friend or relative to help. Maybe they know someone who would be willing to dress up and drive for the day!

♥ . . . . ♥

Tip: Don't be tempted to drive yourself, especially if you and your fiancé are traveling together, unless you absolutely have to. The bride, or bridal couple, is the last to arrive — all the nearby parking spots will be taken!

♥ . . . . ♥

Family Car

Did you and your fiancé go on your first dates in the old family car? Perhaps it holds romantic memories for you both. Why not polish up the old station wagon or pick up truck and dress it up with ribbons and flowers?

Horse and Carriage

I cannot tell you how many times I have heard brides tell me that they dream of arriving at their wedding in a horse and buggy. This much loved means of transport can be an ideal choice if you live outside a major metropolitan area. It can, however, become expensive. Ask around your neighborhood and call horse riding schools — they may be able to put you in touch with someone in the horse community who may be able to help.

Use Your Imagination

Why not try something completely different? How about arriving on a bicycle made for two or a moped — if your dress allows! Let your imagination run wild and you will think of something.

Out of Town Guests

It would be extremely helpful, not to mention considerate, to arrange transportation for out of town guests. Because they may be paying for flights as well as hotels it is a lot to expect that they rent cars as well.

Talk to members of your wedding party — parents, attendants, groomsmen — and allocate pick ups and drop offs. You may even want to arrange tours of your hometown.

Designated Drivers

If anyone volunteers to be a designated driver after your reception, be sure to thank their good sense by supplying an adequate choice of non-alcoholic drinks at your reception. If you are serving alcohol, someone will have to drive — and designated drivers are all too often forgotten.

You can cut down the number of designated drivers required, by hiring or borrowing a minibus or large van, which will carry more people than a car.

CHAPTER ELEVEN

. . . .

The Reception

Eat, drink and be merry

What type of reception do you and your fiancé imagine? Does it fit into your budget or do you need to be a little creative? If you follow some of the suggestions and ideas covered in this chapter, you will see how to have any style reception on any size budget!

I have included some menu suggestions for each type of reception.

Choosing the Type of Reception

If you plan to have your reception immediately after the ceremony, the style will be influenced by the time of day during which you hold your service. However, if you prefer, there is absolutely no reason why you could not be married in the morning, then wait until evening for your reception. This leaves you the time in between to enjoy with your new husband and both families.

To help you decide what you would like to do, write a list of essentials, including:

- ♥ Cake
- ♥ Champagne (or sparkling wine)
- ♥ Lunch
- ♥ Dinner
- ♥ Toasts
- ♥ Speeches
- ♥ Music
- ♥ Dancing

Check anything that you feel is essential to having the reception you really want. Add to the list and prioritize everything on it until you can clearly see what is really important, what is less so and what you could cut out, depending upon the cost.

Brunch Reception

If your choice is an early morning wedding, follow it with a brunch reception. A brunch could be hosted at pretty much any venue, either self-catered or served by a hotel or restaurant, and would involve less organization than an evening reception, for example, where guests generally expect to eat more, drink more and maybe follow the meal with dancing.

Brunch Menu Suggestions:

- • Hearty breakfast buffet — biscuits and gravy, bacon, sausage and eggs

- Pancakes and syrup
- Breakfast fajitas
- Cold cuts, cheeses and a selection of breads
- Croissants and Danish pastries
- Bagels and cream cheese
- Scrambled eggs and salmon
- Kedgeree

Kedgeree:
Ingredients for 10 guests:
2 lbs smoked haddock
2 lemons (sliced)
1 sprig fresh parsley
4 tablespoons butter
1 cup chopped onions
1lb long grain rice
2 pints fish stock
4 hard boiled eggs

Put the fish, lemon and parsley into a large pan and cover with water. Bring to a boil, lower the heat and simmer until the fish is tender. Drain the fish, remove the lemon, parsley, skin and bones. Flake the fish. Melt the butter in a deep pan and fry the chopped onion gently for five minutes. Add the rice and fish stock. Boil then simmer for 20 minutes. Slice three of the hard-boiled eggs. Stir the sliced eggs and flaked fish gently into the rice. Add salt and pepper to taste. Garnish with the remaining egg and fresh parsley. Serve with heart shaped toast.

Any of these would be beautifully complemented by serving coffee, fruit juice and mimosas (sparkling wine and orange juice). Wedding cake could also be served.

It is possible to serve around 50 guests with some of these menu ideas for less than $30! Remember to shop around — some places, for example, offer free cream cheese with bagels, others double up for free. Wherever possible, shop at wholesale clubs, too. If you don't belong to one, look out for trial membership coupons in your Sunday newspaper. This could help to bring your price down even lower!

Lunch Buffet

A lunch buffet can be served either hot or cold. Similar to the brunch, the reception will generally be shorter. In addition to coffee, fruit juice and mimosas, you may choose to serve wine and beer. If you and your family are preparing the food, keeping it simple will ensure a successful meal, enjoyed by everyone.

Maybe you or your fiancé have family from somewhere else around the world. Why not incorporate something from this culture into your menu?

Hot menus:

- *Italian:* Dishes of different pastas, with choice of sauces such as bolognase, carbonara or pesto. Provide with giant dishes of lasagna. Delicious when served with mixed green salads and Italian breads.
- *Mexican:* Tacos and fajitas. Serve all ingredients in separate dishes so that guests can fill their own. Add side dishes of tortilla chips and dips.
- *British:* Shepherd's pie, chicken casserole or beef stew. Serve with corn, peas and baby carrots and bread.
- *Chinese:* Stir fried chicken and vegetables, sweet and sour pork, served with fried rice. Add spring rolls, fried wontons and fortune cookies.

- **American:** Barbecue ribs (watch your dress!), burgers and hot dogs. Serve with baked beans, coleslaw and fries. Alternatively, if you have traditional regional dishes, choose them.
- **Indian:** Curry and rice, with nan bread and popadums. There are so many varieties of curry, I recommend checking a recipe book before choosing which to serve.

Cold Menus:
Mix and match any or all of the following:

- Whole roast turkey (to be carved by guests or one designated person)
- Cold cuts of meat
- Cold salads: potato salad, coleslaw, pasta salad, mixed green salad, Caesar salad
- Mixed cheeses
- Breads and crackers
- Fruit, cookies and cakes
- Variety of finger sandwiches
- Nuts, chips and dips

Lunch at a Hotel or Restaurant

If your guest list is not too long, you can also host a lunch at a hotel or restaurant. If you book far enough in advance, most restaurants will set up pretty much any size table.

Discuss the menu beforehand and select a few dishes which fit into your budget. This way, your guests will still have a choice in what they eat, but be limited to the menu items which you have chosen.

There is no need to serve anything stronger than wine, beer or champagne.

Afternoon Tea

This can be either a simple, yet elegant, afternoon tea, or a full tea dance with a band playing background music. Tea, soft drinks, wine, beer, punch and champagne can all be served.

Afternoon Tea Menus:

- Variety of finger sand-
  wiches
- Cookies
- Cakes and pastries
- Fruit salad and ice cream
- Hot buttered crumpets

Dinner

Again, here you may choose, if you have a long guest list, to prepare the food with the help of friends and family. It is certainly the most fun and economical way to do it! Alternatively, if you have a shorter guest list, you may want to go with a restaurant, in the same fashion as I described for a lunch.

Semi-Professional Caterers

A professionally catered reception can become extremely expensive, with prices charged per head. A great way to get professional standard catering, at a fraction of the cost, is to use students from a catering college. They can provide an exquisitely catered hot or cold meal, using the college facilities. Most catering students will also act as wait staff during the reception, too.

Pot Luck

A pot luck dinner is a wonderful option, especially if you have a few great cooks on your guest list! Stick to asking your closest friends or family for help, if you can. Choose one person, preferably one who will not be too involved in other things on the wedding day, to coordinate everything. They will need to keep on top of:

- Who is bringing what dish
- When it should be brought
- Where it needs to be stored
- Setting the food out on the table
- Sorting out any last minute glitches

Many of the brides I interviewed for this book chose to serve a pot luck dinner at their reception. Without exception, they all agreed that it worked beautifully; they were also all complimented afterwards for the delicious selection of foods served!

Accepting Help

If you are planning a large reception, don't be afraid to ask for help! The work is fun and everyone will enjoy having the opportunity to be involved. A good team of volunteers — and only accept help from those you know *really* want to do it and have the time to spare — can make the day run smoothly and ease any stress. Perhaps you could ask people you know and trust, but who would not be attending the wedding, to act as wait staff or entertain children.

♥ . . . . ♥

Tip: Consider bartering labor. Do you know anyone else who is getting married? Ask them to act as waiters or bar keepers and return the favor at their wedding. A bride that I interviewed repaid her helpers by baby-sitting!

♥ . . . . ♥

Where to Hold the Reception

Unless you are holding your wedding service and reception at the same location, you will need to decide on a venue. Once you know approximately how many guests will be coming and what type of reception you wish to hold, you can start shopping around. Local hotels can become quite competitive, so collect quotes from several — and don't forget to let them know that you are doing this. They may be prepared to offer extras in order to win your business! The same goes for restaurants.

Chambers of Commerce and Visitors' and Convention Bureaus

A visit to your local Chamber of Commerce and Visitors' and Convention Bureau can turn up some wonderful suggestions. Both offices deal with local businesses and are generally extremely knowledgeable about them.

Party Rental Services

If you are holding your reception at home, in a park, in a garden or anywhere else that may have a shortage of tables and chairs, visit as many party rental stores as you can. Prices vary dramatically from one to another.

You will be able to rent anything you need from tables and chairs to linens and tableware.

Wholesale Clubs

Wholesale clubs sell a whole lot more than just foods. Not only are they great places to buy the food, and some of the drinks for your reception, but they also offer a variety of paper napkins, table coverings and disposable tableware, which you will need, too.

Decorating Tables

It is entirely a matter of personal taste how you decorate your tables. Some people prefer traditional wedding decor while others prefer something a little out of the ordinary. There are numerous less traditional ideas for table decorating, which are inexpensive and effective! I have covered some for you in the next few paragraphs.

For the Bridal Party

If you would like to dress up the chairs that the bridal party will be sitting on, drape them with white tulle (fine net) and tie it in place around the back of the chair with ribbon to match the bride's dress. I would recommend avoiding colored ribbon — all it takes is a small amount of liquid spilt on it, for the color to run on your dress!

Themes

Using a specific theme for a reception is becoming an increasingly popular idea.

There is no reason why you have to decorate with just candles and flowers! Are you great travelers? How about having each table decorated to reflect a different country around the world? Maybe you are going skiing for your honeymoon — make a small mountain scene for the center of each table. I heard from one couple, who chose 1930's style clothes for themselves and their attendants. They decorated their reception hall using a gangster theme and suggested that their guests dress to match! Another couple were moving to Hawaii. All their guests turned up in brightly colored shirts, shorts or sarongs, and wore leis. The tables were decorated to match and all the drinks (including beer) were served with drinking straws and umbrellas in them!

Hosted Tables

Have one responsible member of your family, or a close friend, "host" each table. Give them a budget to spend, and tell them what the wedding colors are — and let them surprise you. Each table's decor will be unique, but remain within the weddings color scheme.

Food Tables

If you are serving a buffet, try to spread the food out on more than one table, to avoid a long line. Alternatively, arrange it so that foods are duplicated on each side of a long table. This way you can have two lines served at one time.

If you are having plenty of dishes set out, you won't have much room for decorations. Instead, to make the table look more appealing, raise some dishes to a slightly higher level. You can do this by wrapping something solid — a small, sturdy box will do — in fabric to match your table cloth. Put this in the middle of the table and place a dish on top.

Tip: If you are having several smaller tables, for example, one holding savory foods, one for sweets, and another for drinks, have members of your family greet guests there, instead of in a receiving line. Your parents can be at one table, your fiancé's parents at another and your attendants at yet another. This will give everyone more time to chat and get to know the guests (not to mention more time to receive the guests' compliments!).

Speeches

Decide well in advance whether you are having long speeches or just a brief toast to the bride and groom. Anyone making a speech or giving a toast will need time to practice what they wish to say!

Traditions vary from culture to culture. In some countries, the father of the bride makes a long speech, followed by the groom and the best man. Traditionally, the bride's father and the groom make speeches which are generally serious in nature, while the best man's, which comes last, is not always in the best possible taste! In other countries, guests are invited to share an anecdote or say a few words about the bride or groom, or both. Another tradition is to cut out the long speeches and ask the maid of honor and best man to each propose a toast to the newly married couple.

Whatever you decide, it is also a great opportunity to thank everyone publicly for there help.

The Wedding Cake

Have you ever been at a wedding where the cake is perfectly cut and served only moments after the bride and groom have stopped smooshing it into each other's faces?

Have you ever wondered how they manage to cut such perfect little squares from a round cake? You have probably never even thought about it! The trick is to use a dummy cake for the cutting. One layer is actual cake — the layer that is cut —while the rest is made of Styrofoam, decorated to match! Meanwhile, out in the kitchen, (or a backroom), a sheet cake has already been cut up and put onto the appropriate number of plates, ready to serve to the guests! A simple idea, but a great way to cut the cost!

If your guest list is small, you may decide to use a sheet cake, which can be made to the size you need, instead of a traditional wedding cake. I tried this at my own wedding. We served a beautiful rectangular chocolate cake, decorated with iced white roses. After we had cut it, we served it to the guests ourselves. We bought it at our local grocery store — for less than $15!

Drinks

When deciding what to serve, take into account the likes of your guests. Although you may have beliefs that stop you from drinking alcohol, consider whether it is fair to expect your guests to follow suit. Equally, you may thoroughly enjoy a good drink or two, but know that some guests don't touch a drop. Be sure to cater to everyone's needs and provide plenty of choices in soft drinks and juices, especially if children will be attendending.

Open Bar

Serving an open bar can become extremely expensive if you plan to serve hard liquor. Why not keep it to wine, beer and sodas only? If you give an opportunity for people to drink free cocktails, they will. Admit it, most of us have been guilty of exactly that!

If you are hosting the reception anywhere that you can supply drinks yourselves, buy boxed wines and decant them into pitchers or decanters, and put them in the middle of each table. A keg of beer may be more economical than bottles, although it does have to be finished! Again, serve it in pitchers.

Check with your liquor store to see if they have a sale or return policy. You may be able to return any unopened bottles for a refund. The store may also supply glasses free of charge.

Cash Bar

In many countries a cash bar is absolutely normal at weddings, no matter how expensive or extravagant the event is. Over here, though, people tend to be a little squeamish about them. The rea-

soning behind this is, if you invite people as guests, you should provide everything for them. Consider, though, that the guests are coming to celebrate a serious event — your marriage service — and not
just to enjoy a huge party! A lot of the financial burden is taken
away if guests are prepared to buy their own drinks.

If you still don't feel comfortable about a cash bar, supply the
wine, beer and sodas, but let guests pay for more exotic drinks.

Remember, only have a cash bar if your reception is at a hotel or
restaurant!

Designated Drivers

Before finishing the subject of drinks, I have one last plug to
make for the designated drivers for the night. Anyone who has vol-
unteered not to drink at your wedding reception, in order to help
other guests home safely, should, at the very least, be rewarded by a
good choice of sodas, tea and coffee!

Music

Music can be an important part of the reception. If you love to
dance, you will want to have music that everyone can get up and
dance to. If you prefer a romantic string quartet to set the tone,
choose that instead.

Look back to your fantasy list. What did you write down there?
Now look at your priority list to see how much you allocated for
music and how important it is to you and your fiancé. This should
give you a better idea of what to look for.

Bands

Visit local bars and coffee shops which host live bands. Many
semi-professional or part time bands play at nights. Aside from
often being extremely talented, their fees are usually considerably
less than a professional group.

Try community choirs or bands, and college choirs. Here you will find amateur musicians, who play beautifully.

Disk Jockeys

Word of mouth is a great recommendation. Ask around. Do you know anyone who used a DJ at their wedding? Were they pleased? Did they feel that they got good value for their money? Did the DJ play all the songs they requested?

Check your local paper for advertisements. You may be able to find a part-time DJ for a lower cost. But be sure to ask for a sample tape and references, before you book anyone!

Contracts

When you have decided on the band or DJ, make sure that everything you agree to is put in writing. Check your agreement for:

- Special equipment needs
- Overtime
- Breaks
- Will they play the music you have requested?

If your reception is going to last several hours, you cannot expect a band to play the entire time without a break. Be sure to provide them with refreshments during their break — and let them know ahead of time that you will do this. It would be a good idea to arrange for some pre-recorded music to be played during the break times.

It is not unreasonable to expect a DJ to stay at his post for a couple of hours, as he will not be starting until after the food has been served. Make sure that he also has a supply of liquid refreshment during the evening.

Choosing the Music

Think about music that will appeal to all the guests, whatever their age group, as well as you and your fiancé. A mix of romantic, show tunes, pop and ethnic should pretty much please everyone.

The First Dances

Traditionally the bride and groom start the dancing by sharing their first dance as a married couple. The song they dance to is usually a sentimental love song, one that is significant to their relationship. They are joined by other members of the bridal party and guests in this order:

- Bride and groom start.
- Bride dances with her father, while the groom dances with the bride's mother.
- Bride dances with the groom's father, while the groom dances with his mother.
- The attendants join in, dancing with each other or their spouses or partners.
- The rest of the guests join in.

Children

If you are having children at the wedding and reception, you will need to arrange some entertainment for them — if you don't want them getting bored and fractious, that is! You may also choose to have someone specifically there to help with the children. At a wedding I attended recently, one of the guests "donated" her nanny for the day. For a very reasonable fee, a responsible adult was on hand to watch the children and keep them entertained, leaving the parents free to relax and enjoy themselves. The children all had a great time — and their parents did too!

Supplying a grab bag of "goodies" for children is also a great way to keep them occupied.   Try some of these:

- Modeling dough
- Coloring books and crayons
- Small toys
- Age appropriate games

All of these can be picked up for very little cost at any dollar store, supermarket or wholesale club. Check mail order gift catalogs, too. They will be well worth the investment!

CHAPTER TWELVE

· — · · · · · · · · · · · · · · · · · ·

Honeymoons

Should last a lifetime . . .

*N*ow that you have chosen your dress and flowers, planned the menu for your reception, and found the perfect band, you are completely *exhausted!* All those hours spent cooking and sewing, organizing and decorating have taken their toll. It is now time to talk vacations, or, more specifically, honeymoons! You have certainly earned a break, and with all the money you saved on your wedding, you may be able to afford more than you realized. Maybe you deliberately chose to spend less on the wedding, so that you could enjoy a spectacular honeymoon.

Here is the big surprise — just like your wedding, your honeymoon, no matter where you spend it, need not cost a fortune!

When you originally planned your wedding budget, did you include honeymoon expenses? By following the suggestions throughout this book, you may have saved even more than you expected. Why not allocate that to your honeymoon.

PLANNING A HONEYMOON

What to do

Consider *what* to do, rather than *where* to do it. Is there an activity that you and your fiancé share in common. Do you both share a great love of mountains, big cities or the beach? Discuss all the options before the two of you decide where to spend your honeymoon.

Because you have decided that you want to spend your lives together, you should be pretty familiar with each other's interests! In the months leading up to the wedding, though, you may have been so wrapped up in the planning and organization, that you had little or no time to indulge any of them. It is easy to forget! Take a night off from wedding planning and promise not to discuss anything about it, other than the honeymoon. Take the opportunity to remind each other of all the shared activities you enjoy and how much you have in common.

Local Honeymoons

No one said you had to travel around the world for your honeymoon. If you live in a state that you both love, and which offers everything you are looking for in your honeymoon, why travel farther afield? Not only will you save the airfares, but, if you drive, you will have the flexibility of a car.

Visit your local travel office or call the state's Visitors' and Convention Bureau, and ask their advice. They will send you packages of information, which will help you choose. You may find that there are parts of your state which you never knew about, yet would love to visit!

Long-Distance Honeymoons

With so many airlines offering discounted flights and two-for-one fares, you have a great opportunity to visit other parts of the country. You may be looking for a complete change of climate. A couple from central Texas did this. Because they didn't see much snow where they live, following their winter wedding, they flew up to Vermont and spent a glorious week throwing snowballs at each other. They took the time to shop around until they found the best value tickets possible.

Finding bargain tickets is not difficult, especially if you are flexible about where you go. To help find them, follow these suggestions:

1. ***Develop a good relationship with a travel agent.*** When they are "personally" involved, you may find they take more time to shop around for you. *Please note:* there are some terrific agents out there who will do this no matter what.

2. ***Check the internet.*** You will be amazed at how many bargains are advertised. If you don't have internet access, book on-line time at your local library. Ask the library staff to show you what to do.

3. **Check rail and bus companies.** Some advertise "specials" such as travel anywhere in the continental U.S. for a one-off price. Others offer companion fares, in which one of you travels free of charge, when the other buys a full price ticket.
4. **Ask around!** Talk to anyone you know who may travel frequently. Contact visitors' bureaus and ask for their advice and suggestions.
5. **Check for sales.** Look in local papers for bargains.

International Honeymoons

If you are planning a long-distance honeymoon, why limit yourselves to the United States? Go international! If you are fortunate enough to live close to one of the borders, an international trip may involve little more than a short drive. If you live further away, shop around for a flight, train, or bus ride.

Other than peak holiday seasons, such as Christmas, you can find bargain flights to almost anywhere in the world. Flights to Europe are particularly good value. Have you ever dreamed of spending a spring honeymoon in Paris? How about a summer trip to London? Oktoberfests in Germany are pretty amazing, too. Economical rail fares throughout the United Kingdom and Europe also bring travel from city to city within your reach.

Don't be put off by the thought that accommodation will be astronomically expensive, either. Most towns and cities in Europe, for example, have hostels where you can stay for an unbelievably low cost. Check with the country's embassy or consulate and ask for their guidance. Every office that I have ever dealt with — and I travel as much as possible — has been extraordinarily helpful. Some will even give you addresses of tourist offices in each local area, where you can write for even more specific information, such as lists of accommodations and prices.

All Inclusive Packages

If you have not already planned your wedding, or you started and decided that eloping was the best option, why not think about an all inclusive wedding/honeymoon package? Just turn up on the appropriate day, with the necessary paperwork, in whatever dress (or shorts or bathing suit) you choose. Everything from the flowers to the cake to the photographs and video will be taken care of for you! All you need to do is sit back and relax and enjoy your honeymoon. The one price you paid will generally cover everything except souvenirs. You won't even have to buy yourselves a celebratory cocktail - it is all covered!

Of course, the downside of all inclusive wedding/honeymoons, is that either you have no guests at your wedding or no privacy for your honeymoon!

What to Pack

Wherever you decide to go, be it a weekend camping, a short drive from your home, or a trip around the world, there are certain things you will need to remember. We all know of someone who has a honeymoon disaster story to tell because they forgot to pack something. How many of us entered this world because one of our parents forgot to pack their birth control! I have friends who booked a week long cruise for their honeymoon. They forgot to pack sunscreen and were so badly sunburnt, they could not touch each other for the whole week!

Here are a few necessities to remember — but, depending on where you go, you may need to add to this list:

- Birth control
- Medications you are currently taking
- Allergy, diarrhea and headache tablets
- Travel sickness medication

- Sunscreen (even if you are going in search of snow!)
- Tickets and passports (if necessary)
- Appropriate clothing
- Something sexy (and your imagination!)

Postponing your Honeymoon

There is no law — or etiquette book, for that matter — that says you have to take your honeymoon immediately after your wedding. In some cases, it may be better to postpone it. My husband and I were a perfect example of this. Because of his military commitments, we were unable to take a honeymoon right away. We both love to ski, so although we were married at the end of April, we did not take our honeymoon until the following December, when we were able to drive to Colorado and share an incredible week together. It was certainly worth the wait!

You may decide to follow our example, not because you have commitments on your time, but because you have just paid for your wedding and are starting a new home together. The first year in a new home can involve a surprising number of unexpected expenses. Why not wait a while, build your home and then take the break you both deserve?

No matter when, where or how you spend it, during your honeymoon, the two of you will share some precious days, or weeks, of your married life. That in itself is enough to guarantee an idyllic vacation. Use it to set the tone of your entire marriage! Your honeymoon should last a lifetime!

CHAPTER THIRTEEN

· ·

The Ceremony

Time to say "I Do"

The day you have had such a wonderful time planning and arranging has finally arrived! Hopefully you managed to get some sleep before you have to leap out of bed, rush to the mirror and check to see if the huge pimple you had nightmares about actually appeared on your nose! It didn't, of course, so you know it is going to be a perfect day!

Pre-Wedding Timetable

The Night Before:

❏ Take a long soak in a scented tub, shave your legs and tweeze your eyebrows.

119

❑ If you are wearing your hair up for the wedding, wash it now. It will hold better if it is just a tiny bit dirty.

❑ Paint your nails or give yourself a manicure.

❑ Get an early night and try to avoid more than a glass of wine — especially if it shows on your face! You want to be looking and feeling your best in the morning.

The Morning of the Wedding:

❑ Try to eat a good breakfast. If you are as nervous as most brides, whatever you put in your mouth will taste like cardboard. So, eat anything; you may not get another chance to eat before the reception — and you certainly don't want to pass out during the service!

❑ Take a shower early — everyone else in your family will be hogging it later.

❑ Finish any last minute tasks for the wedding, such as arranging your bouquet or picking up the cake.

❑ Double check everything!

❑ Have your hair done, if you are getting it styled at a salon, even if your wedding is late in the day. Unless the weather is extremely humid or it is raining, it will hold perfectly. In most cases, your style will need to drop a little, anyway.

Getting Ready:

❑ Ask your maid of honor and bridesmaids to arrive at least a couple of hours before the service. You will have plenty to chat about while you get ready!

❑ Do each other's hair and make up — and remember, this is not the time to experiment with a new look!

❑ Get dressed!

❑ Enjoy a little time with your parents before the pre-wedding photographs are taken.

❑ Have one fortifying glass of champagne and a toast to your parents and attendants, before leaving for the service.

❑ Move your engagement ring to your right hand. You can return it to your left hand after the service.

Make Up:

If you want to look like the archetypal blushing bride, steer clear of dark, heavy make ups. The best look for a bride and her attendants is to keep it as natural as possible. Try different styles and colors well in advance.

A great way to try out wedding make-up is to visit a department store cosmetic stand and ask the assistant to show you what they have in bridal colors. They will be happy to demonstrate their cosmetics on you and teach you how to achieve the same look yourself. Some department stores even give out coupons for brides and one attendant specifically for this.

Tip: If you are changing brands of cosmetics or changing your beauty regimen, do this several weeks before the wedding. You don't want to find yourself with an allergic reaction and a red, puffy face!

Relax!!

I know it is almost impossible — your hands will be shaking and you won't be able to keep your breakfast down — but do try to relax before the wedding ceremony. It is a wonderful experience and not the terrifying ordeal some people hype it up to be!

Try a little yoga, or at the very least take some deep breaths! You are meant to be enjoying yourself!

Bride's Attendants

Decide whether they are all getting ready with you or meeting you at the service site. If you are going to meet up at the site, make sure that everyone knows how to get there and what time they need to arrive.

Groom and Groomsmen

Lucky guys — they have nothing more challenging to do than get showered, shaved and dressed, before leaving for the church or wedding site!

Ushers

The ushers need to arrive at the site at least an hour before the ceremony. They can check that all the flowers are in place and be there to welcome any early guests. Closer to the time of the service, they will be busy welcoming guests and showing them to their seats.

When the bride and her attendants are ready, the ushers will show first the mother of the groom and then the mother of the bride to their seats. This is the signal that the wedding is about to start.

Divorced Parents

This can be a sticky problem if there is any acrimony between divorced parents. We have all laughed at movies where the bride's parents show up and ruin the whole event. It may be hilarious in the movies, but who really wants it to happen at their own wedding! Hopefully, any divorced parents will respect the importance of the day and behave accordingly.

If you have any concerns, take time to talk to both parties before the wedding. Tell them how much it means to you that they put the past behind them and set aside any differences, if only for one day.

Of course, if all else fails, you can always seat them as far apart as possible!

THE SERVICE

You arrive at the site of the service. The guests are seated. So what do you do now?

Often it all remains a mystery until the rehearsal. What do you do when you arrive at the church? What do you say once you have walked up the aisle? We have all been to different weddings at some time or another and although we have a vague recollection of the words used, we rarely remember them exactly.

To complicate things even more, there are no longer set vows. Most ministers will personalize vows for each couple. Many couples have chosen to write their own vows.

But, whether your wedding is religious or civil, traditional or modern, the vows you exchange will be the most moving and beautiful part of the entire wedding. This is the heart of the service.

Examples of Services

There are so many permutations of the marriage service, it would be impossible for me to cover them all. In fact, I could fill an entire book with them! Instead, I have given examples of one christian service, one Jewish service, one civil and one where the couple wrote their own vows for their completely untraditional — but incredibly moving — marriage service. I apologize to any reader who would have liked their particular branch of the church to be the one included.

The services described in this chapter are all actual services that have been held and can be used as examples. They will, of course, vary depending on exactly where you are getting married and who the officiant is.

No matter what your religion, I suggest that you discuss the service in great depth with your minister, priest, rabbi, etc. They will be able to address any specific questions you have.

Christian Service

Because the example illustrated is the favorite choice for couples married at the Wilton Baptist Church, in upstate New York, I have not included specific names.

The Processional

The groom stands nervously at the alter, the organist starts the music and you take your father's arm. You are ready to take the longest walk of your life!

In some cultures the bride's attendants walk ahead of her up the aisle, in others they follow. They can walk up in single file or in pairs. It is a matter of personal choice.

When the minister gives you the signal to start, you will walk up the aisle towards your groom. Traditionally, a bride walks on her father's right hand side, so that she stands to the left of the groom, when she reaches the altar. This tradition dates back to the times when a groom would need to have his right hand free to wield his sword, in case anyone tried to steal his bride back! Because this doesn't happen a lot these days, if you prefer to break with tradition and stand on your groom's right — go ahead. I did!

Where Does Everyone Stand?

This is usually up to the officiant. Discuss it with him or her first, though, you may prefer a different arrangement from the one suggested. Generally, the maid of honor stands to the left of the bride, while the best man stands to the right of the groom. The bridesmaids stand a little to one side, the groomsmen or ushers to the other. For the duration of the ceremony, the maid of honor holds the bride's bouquet for her. In some cases, the minister may take the bride's bouquet and place it on the altar until the recessional. He can discreetly retrieve it while the newly married couple share a kiss.

Giving of the Bride

The minister will ask who gives the bride in marriage to the groom. Your father, or whoever is 'giving you away' (you may prefer to think of it as whoever escorted you up the aisle!) will respond by saying "I do," or perhaps, "Her mother and I do."

A popular alternative:

The pastor asks the bride's father, "(Father's full name), by walking your daughter (bride's full name) down the aisle, are you affirming that both you and your wife are giving your full blessing to the marriage of your daughter to this man? Are you also hereby transferring your God given responsibility of the care and the protection of your daughter to this man?"

The father replies, "We are."

The pastor tells him, "Then you may kiss your daughter as a symbol that you are transferring the care and protection of your daughter to (groom's name)."

After the father kisses his daughter, the pastor asks, "Who giveth this woman to be married to this man?"

The father responds, "I do."

At this point in most weddings, the father steps aside and joins the bride's mother in the front pew.

Exchange of Vows

The pastor asks the groom, "(groom's first name), do you, in the presence of this pastor and these people, and in the sight of God, take (bride's first name) to be your wedded wife? Do you promise to strive to love her even as Christ loved the church and gave himself for it? Do you vow a love that will always seek her good and bring glory to God?"

The groom responds, "I do."

The pastor asks the bride, "(bride's first name), Do you, in the presence of this pastor and these people, and in the sight of God, take (groom's first name) to be your wedded husband? Do you promise to strive to love him even as Christ loved you and gave himself for you? Do you vow a love that will always seek his good and bring glory to God?"

The bride responds, "I do."

Ring Ceremony

The officiant will ask for the rings at the appropriate time in the service. The best man can either carry both in his pocket, or he may carry the bride's ring, which he passes to the groom, while the maid of honor carries the groom's ring, which she passes to the bride. The wedding rings are blessed and you place them on the third finger of each other's left hand.

Have you ever seen a couple exchange the rings without fumbling? You will probably do exactly the same, so don't worry! Your hands will be shaking from the heady mixture of excitement and emotion!

Hymns, Prayers and Readings

You may choose to have hymns sung, especially if your service is in church. If so, you will also want to join the minister in prayers and perhaps include a reading or sermon. There is absolutely no reason why you cannot do any of these outside a church, either.

Some time before the wedding, your officiant will be able to supply you with a book of hymns, from which he can recommend a selection of appropriate choices.

Unless you know a particular prayer that you would like used, your officiant will be able to select the prayers on your behalf. The same goes for readings or a sermon. If you already have a choice piece — for either the officiant, a relative or a friend to read — be sure to discuss working it into the program ahead of time.

The Kiss...

It has long been a tradition that when the minister has pronounced the couple married, the maid of honor lifts the bride's veil and rearranges it so that the groom may kiss his new wife.

The Recessional

The bride and groom walk back down the aisle, arm in arm or holding hands. They are followed by the best man and maid of honor. The other attendants pair up behind them. After the attendants, come the bride's mother, on the arm of the groom's father, and the bride's father, holding the arm of the groom's mother.

When the wedding party has left the church, all the guests are at liberty to leave, too.

Jewish Service

There are no set rules as far as a Jewish wedding is concerned because of the differences between the four branches of the faith; Orthodox, Conservative, Reform and Reconstructionist. There are, however, numerous traditions that are used in most weddings.

Ketuvah

The Jewish ceremony starts with the signing of the ketuvah, a document detailing the husband's obligations to his wife. The groom signs, together with two adult male witnesses, neither of whom should be related to either the bride or groom.

Bedekin

The tradition of bedekin, veiling, is now being dropped from many weddings. For those couples who still choose to go with it, the groom, together with his father and soon-to-be father-in-law, visit the room where the bride greets her guests, to see that she is indeed the correct bride. When this has been confirmed, the groom covers his bride's face with her veil.

The Processional

The bride walks up the aisle, flanked by her parents. Halfway up, the groom meets them, together with his parents, and accompanies them the rest of the way to the chuppah, a decorated canopy under which the marriage ceremony takes place.

The Service

The service starts with the rabbi or officiant reciting a blessing over a cup of wine. The bride and groom then sip from the cup. An example of this blessing is:

"Oh God, supremely blessed, supreme in might and glory, guide and bless this groom and bride, standing here in the presence of God, the guardian of the home, ready to enter into the bond of wedlock."

This blessing is followed by the exchange of rings, the centerpiece of the service. The rabbi instructs the couple, "Answer in the fear of God, and in the hearing of those assembled."

The rabbi asks the groom, "Do you, (groom), of your own free will and consent, take (bride) to be your wife? And do you promise to love, honor and cherish her throughout life?"

The groom responds, "I do."

The rabbi then asks the bride, "Do you, (bride), of your own free will and consent, take (groom) to be your husband? And do you promise to love, honor and cherish him throughout life?"

The bride responds, "I do."

Sheva B'rachot

Sheva b'rachot are the seven blessings given over a second cup of wine. They can be read by the rabbi or by honored guests.

"You abound in blessings, Adonai our God, who created the fruit of the vine."

"You abound in blessings, Adonai our God. You created all things for your glory."

"You abound in blessings, Adonai our God. You made humankind in your image, after your likeness, and you prepared for us a perpetual relationship. You abound in blessings, Adonai our God. You created humanity."

"May she who was barren rejoice when her children are united in her midst in joy. You abound in blessings, Adonai our God, who makes Zion rejoice with her children."

"You make those beloved companions greatly rejoice, even as you rejoiced in your creation of Eden, as of old. You abound in blessings, Adonai our God, who makes the bridegroom and bride rejoice."

"You abound in blessings, Adonai our God, who created joy and gladness, bridegroom and bride, mirth and exultation, pleasure and delight, love, fellowship, peace and friendship."

"Soon may there be heard in the cities of Judah and in the cities of Jerusalem, the voice of joy and gladness, the voice of the bridegroom, the voice of the bride, the jubilant voices of bridegrooms from their canopies and of youths from their feasts of song. You abound in blessings, Adonai our God. You make the bridegroom rejoice with the bride."

At this point the couple once again sip from the cup of wine, and the rabbi pronounces them married. Traditionally the groom then breaks a glass by stamping on it, to symbolize the destruction of the temple in Jerusalem. Less traditional couples prefer to break the glass together.

Civil Service

The following civil service was the one that my husband and I chose. The officiant was a Justice of the Peace. Guests stood in a semi-circle and sipped champagne with the groom until the bride arrived.

♥ ARNO'S AND DI'S WEDDING ♥

Justice of the Peace says, *"We are gathered here on this 29th day of April to witness the joining in holy matrimony of Arno and Di, and by the authority of a license issued by the officials of the State of Texas, I announce that this union is sanctioned and duly authorized.*

If any person can show cause or reason why this couple may not be lawfully joined and wedded, let them speak now or forever hold their peace and remain silent.

Arno, do you take this woman Di to be your lawfully wedded wife? Do you promise to love her, comfort her, honor and keep her, in sickness and in health, and do you promise to forsake all others, and keep yourself only unto her for so long as you both shall live?"

Arno responds, *"I do."*

"Di, do you take Arno to be your lawfully wedded husband? Do you promise to love him, comfort him, honor and keep him, in sickness and in health, and do you promise to forsake all others and keep yourself only unto him for as long as you both shall live?"

Di responds, *"I do."*

Ring Ceremony

Justice of the Peace says to the groom, *"Place the ring on her finger and repeat after me saying to her: with this ring I thee wed and I pledge my love to you and may this ring symbolize my love and my fidelity."* Arno repeats.

Justice of the Peace says to the bride, *"Place the ring on his finger and repeat after me saying to him: with this ring I thee wed and I pledge my love to you and may this ring symbolize my love and my fidelity."* Di repeats.

Justice of the Peace says, *"For as much as you both have consented and agreed to join together in this sacred covenant of marriage and accordingly have pledged to each other your faith, your trust and your love, I pronounce you husband and wife."*

Writing Your Own Vows

Increasingly, couples are steering away from the more formal vows and choosing to write their own. This can be an incredibly moving and personal experience.

♥ JANET'S AND JOHN'S WEDDING ♥

Guests formed a circle in the garden. The service started with an introduction by the minister.

"Good afternoon! On behalf of Janet and John, I welcome you to this place and this happy event. We have come from the four corners of the nation — from Atlanta and Massachusetts and Montana — in response to an absolutely delightful wedding invitation. We are here to celebrate and acknowledge the bond between these two lovely people who are part of our hearts and our lives, and to offer them our loving support. We do not marry them; we are witnesses as they marry each other."

Janet and John each welcome their guests and state their intent, before turning towards the minister.

The minister continues: *"Janet and John, today in the presence of your families and friends, you are celebrating the creation of something utterly unique in the world — your marriage. Because each of you is unique, the marriage you are creating — and will continue to create — is unique. There is nothing quite like it in the history of the world. What you are, what you have, what you will be, is a distinctive treasure.*

We can say, in fact, that the path that has brought you to this garden this day has been a treasure hunt. You have called it a story of hide and seek — starting from your childhood, when you played hide and seek in your neighborhood, here in Rochester, your gaining and losing touch across the years, never quite forgetting the other, until, through many changes, you came together in Rochester again. Though you have changed since you first played hide and seek, many things remain the same. The life that you are leading together had its seeds planted long ago. The treasure you perceived in each other then has grown richer. You marry in the hope that what you have sought for yourself, but have had trouble finding, may be fulfilled through the strengths of the other.

Your game of hide and seek has come to an end, and yet it hasn't. You will still play, hiding in the mystery of individuality and the need for privacy, but always searching for each other in mutual comfort and support, in mutual growth, in absolutely indispensable laughter, in becoming reacquainted again and again. The world's sages have often observed that life's greatest treasures are in hiding, but that they may certainly be found. Seek and you shall find are words familiar to us; may you continue to seek, and may you find treasure that will bless you all your days."

At this point in the service, family and friends were invited to share their feelings with Janet and John.

The minister: *"It is now time for others to do some talking and sharing. Contrary to the usual way in which wedding guests are offered a chance to say something — that is, why the couple should not be married — you have been invited by your wedding invitation to share briefly your thoughts, feelings and talents on such topics as the significance of marriage, your hope for Janet and John as a couple, or simply what you like about them being married. We want you to feel perfectly free to speak (or sing or play or read), or not to. Let me ask the bride's mother, Ann, to start off with the song that she has chosen to share with Janet and John during this time."*

Sharing the Bread of Life

Janet and John chose to use bread, likening its transformation from its early stage as seed and its phases as grain and flour before offering nourishment, to the transformation a man and woman undergo through the experiences of marriage. A loaf of bread was specially prepared for them. After taking a piece each, they passed the loaf around the circle, asking everyone to join them in eating it, as a sign of bonding.

Their Vows

The minister asks, *"Do you two have vows to make to each other?"*

John speaks first, saying, *"Our marriage is a journey that will take the rest of our lives to complete. Let us undertake it joyfully and wholeheartedly, confident that our commitments will never be taken for granted, strong in the knowledge that our dreams for the future are safe in each other's hands, and thankful that all we have learned, and every experience we have encountered, has led us to this place."*

Janet continues, *"May we bring to our marriage the same energy and curiosity we knew in our youth. May our long friendship be a source of tenderness, trust and understanding. If there are times when we stand certain of nothing but our love, let us rely on the stability our history has created. We are fortunate to have the freedom this marriage brings — the freedom to love each other for a lifetime."*

John says, *"I celebrate the joy and intimacy you have brought to my life. I promise to be your life companion, to communicate honestly, to accept you fully as you are and delight in who you are becoming, to encourage your fulfillment, and to compassionately support you through all the changes of your life."*

Janet says, *"I celebrate the joy and intimacy you have brought to my life. I promise to be your life companion, to communicate honestly, to accept you fully as you are and delight in who you are becoming, to encourage your fulfillment, and to compassionately support you through all the changes of your life."*

The Ring Ceremony

Janet, while placing the ring on John's finger says, *"I give you this ring as a symbol of my love."*

John, while placing the ring on Janet's finger says, *"I give you this ring as a symbol of my love."*

The minister declares, *"Janet and John, John and Janet: by the authority vested in me by state and church, and through my friendship with you and your family, I pronounce you to be husband and wife, wife and husband — and may the blessings of the Creator and the in-dwelling spirit of life and love be with you in your journey — which will begin with a kiss..."*

CHAPTER FOURTEEN

· ·

Real Life Budget Brides

How we did it

*W*hen it comes to weddings, you will be amazed at how willing people are to help out. Don't be afraid to ask for their help, and use all the resources available to you. One of the best ways to find great wedding ideas is to talk to those who have *been there, done that.*

This book was written drawing on the successes of brides who planned their weddings with small budgets. Between us, we have covered all styles of weddings, from civil to religious, intimate to large, a handful of guests to a couple of hundred. Some of us spent a couple of hundred dollars, some a couple of thousand. The most expensive wedding between us cost $2000, most of them cost far less.

We have tried everything and had some wonderful experiences along the way. We also made some mistakes and learnt from them. One thing we all agreed on, though — we all enjoyed the wedding of our dreams! Here, a few of us share our personal experiences and actual wedding budgets with you, including anything we would have done differently!

♥ LOIS AND CARL ♥

Invitations: Lois and Carl skipped printed invitations all together and invited their 150 guests by word of mouth.

In hindsight, Lois admitted that she would have preferred to send out formal, written invitations.

The Bride: Lois found a full length ivory prom dress, which suited her perfectly, in a local department store. It was even on clearance! Her headpiece and veil were made as a gift by her mother-in-law. As the wedding was at Christmas time, for her bouquet, she carried a bunch of poinsettias, tied around the stems with ribbon.

The Groom: Carl was fortunate enough to be able to borrow a white tuxedo from his cousin.

Wedding Rings: They bought their wedding rings from a chain store in the mall.

The Attendants: Lois and Carl chose to have just a maid of honor and a best man. The maid of honor supplied her own dress and carried a white muff instead of flowers. The best man wore his own three piece suit.

Flowers and Decorations: The church was already decorated for Christmas, so Lois and Carl needed very little in the way of decorations. There was even a beautifully decorated 12-foot Christmas tree and banks of poinsettias, matching Lois' bouquet. The only addition Lois made to the decor, was to cut small flowering magnolia branches, which she tied with ribbons and attached to the family pews at the front of the church.

The Ceremony: They chose a traditional religious ceremony, which was held in a church.

The Reception: The reception, which followed immediately after the service, at the same church, was a relaxed, informal event. Finger foods, prepared by friends and relatives were served, along with punch. The wedding cake, three-tiered and decorated with tiny poinsettias to continue the theme, was made by Lois' aunt.

Photographs and Video: A cousin, who is a talented photographer, took the formal pictures. Lois and Carl covered the cost of film and developing.

Budget Breakdown:

Marriage License $25
Minister $50
Invitations $0
Ceremony Venue $0
    (included in Minister's fee)
Reception Venue $0
Reception Food $0
    (gift from friends and relatives)
Reception Drinks... $15

Wedding Cake $35
Decorations $10
Flowers $10
Bride's Clothing
    (dress, shoes, headpiece and veil) $65
Groom's Clothing (borrowed Tux) $0
Wedding Rings $120
Attendant's Clothing.. $0
    (supplied their own)
Photographs (film and developing) $40

Total Cost of Wedding: *$370*

♥ **DI AND ARNO** ♥

(This was my own wonderful wedding!)

Invitations: We printed our own at home, using sheets of invitation cards bought from an office supply store.

The Bride: I could not find anything I liked in the stores locally (at least not in my price range!) but was fortunate enough to find the perfect dress pattern and fabric — exactly what I had imagined! The dress was long and fitted, with a lace bodice. I made it in ivory cotton moiré (a heavy fabric that hangs well and has a slight sheen to it). A length of silk tulle had been gathering dust in my sewing box for years, so I dug it out and made my veil from it.

The Groom: As a commissioned officer in the United States Army, Arno was able to wear his uniform. He chose Dress Blues.

Wedding Rings: We found our rings in a department store. We both wanted something simple and symbolic, and found a matching pair of completely plain gold bands.

Attendants: We had a best man — Arno's dad! — maid of honor and one usher — both friends. The best man and usher wore their own clothes, we only gave them a boutonnière. The maid of honor wore a short version of my dress, in emerald green. She supplied the fabric and I made the dress.

Flowers and Decorations: Our wedding was held in a small private rose garden beside a lake — what could we do to improve on that? We planned to add no extra decorations, other than a table we could serve champagne from, but one of the staff at the apartment complex where we lived, and where the wedding took place, surprised us by decorating the benches with paper ribbons.

The roses in the garden were white and I carried a simple bouquet of white stem roses to match. My godmother, who made the bouquet, tied the roses with ivory colored ribbon, to match my dress. We bought two corsages — one for my hair and one for the maid of honor's hair. They were made with white freesias, my late mother's favorite flower.

The boutonnières worn by the best man, the usher, the mother of the groom and my godmother, who gave me away, were single white rosebuds, to match my bouquet, tied with narrow ivory ribbon and attached to clothing by dressmaker pins.

For the reception, which we held in our apartment, we decorated with nothing more than a new white lace tablecloth and plenty of green candles.

The Ceremony: We were married by a Justice of the Peace, in a civil ceremony. The service was intimate and informal, with all the guests standing in a semi-circle around us, sipping champagne!

The Reception: Our reception came in two parts! We started more formally with speeches, toasts and a meal in our apartment, before heading out to a local night club for dancing and cutting the cake.

We served huge dishes of Shepherd's Pie, which I had prepared the day before, along with sweetcorn and homemade bread rolls. Thanks to my mother and father-in-law, there was no shortage of champagne, wine, beer and cocktails!

Our wedding cake came from a local grocery store — a half sheet of chocolate cake, covered with white frosted roses.

Photographs and Video: A friend, who had been a photographer before joining the army, took our formal wedding pictures, while guests took more relaxed shots. They all sent us copies afterwards.

Our advice: don't give your photographer too much champagne before he takes the pictures! As our whole wedding was an easy-going, intimate affair, the last thing we wanted was an intrusive video. Instead, the camera was passed around among the guests, who all had a few words of commentary during their turn!

Budget Breakdown:

Marriage License $31
Justice of Peace $65
Invitations $10
Service Venue $0
Reception Venue $0
Reception Food... $50
Reception Drink.. $200
    (a welcome gift, so we did not
    pay for this ourselves!)

Wedding Cake $12
Decorations.. $20
Flowers (bouquet, headpieces, boutonnières) $60
Bride's Clothing (dress, shoes and veil) $35
Groom's Clothing (military uniform)............................ $0
Wedding Rings $70
Attendant's Clothing $0
    (everyone supplied their own)
Photographs (wedding gift) $0
Video (cost of film).. $5
Music for Dancing...
(the nightclub gave us free admittance!) $0

Total Cost of Wedding: ***$558***

♥ KATHLEEN AND RICHARD ♥

Invitations: Kathleen and Richard wanted to keep their wedding small and intimate — 25 guests — so invited everyone personally. After the wedding, they sent out formal announcements.

The Bride: Kathleen wore a pale apricot colored 1920's era dress, with a three-tiered, mid-calf skirt — which she found in a going out of business sale. With it she wore a wide-brimmed picture hat with a small veil at the front.

The Groom: Richard wore his own suit.

Wedding Rings: Kathleen and Richard chose matching gold bands with detailing around the edges.

Attendants: Kathleen and Richard had a maid of honor and best man, both of whom supplied their own clothing.

Flowers and Decorations: In the way that many girls imagine the fairytale gown they will one day wear, Kathleen had always dreamed of carrying a bouquet of lavender tulips, tied with ribbon! Her dream came true!

The flowers she bought came from San Francisco's flower market — the same market where retail florists buy their flowers. Some stalls were open to the public, so she was able to pick up armfuls of flowers for very little cost. Her uncle, an artist, arranged flowers throughout her parent's house for the reception.

The Ceremony: The marriage service was held in the same park where Richard had first told Kathleen that he loved her! They chose a fairly secluded spot in a semi-circle of redwood trees, at the end of a meadow. Kathleen's brother, a professional classical musician, played music for them on a battery operated keyboard.

The Reception: The reception was held in Kathleen's parents' house, a block and a half walk from the wedding site. For food they served hors d'ouevres, made by family and friends, that could be eaten without utensils. Wine, beer, champagne, sparkling cider, mineral water and sodas were also served.

Kathleen rented glasses from a party supply store and served food on high quality paper plates. All the food was served from platters and baskets friends and family already owned.

Photographs: Kathleen's sister-in-law, whose job involves plenty of photography, took the formal pictures. Kathleen and Richard decided on black and white formal photos, while guests took more candid color pictures.

Budget Breakdown:

Marriage License $69
Minister $225
Announcements $106
Service Venue $0
Reception Venue $0
Reception Food and Drinks $375
Wedding Cake $108
Decorations... $0
Flowers... $35
Bride's Clothing $279
Groom's Clothing.. $0
Wedding Rings... $200
Attendant's Clothing $0
    (they both supplied their own)
Photographs $150
Miscellaneous (glass rental, paperware, ice) $55

Total Cost of Wedding: *$1602*

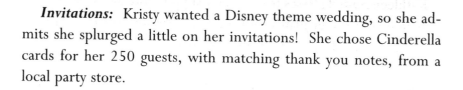

♥ KRISTY AND AARON ♥

Invitations: Kristy wanted a Disney theme wedding, so she admits she splurged a little on her invitations! She chose Cinderella cards for her 250 guests, with matching thank you notes, from a local party store.

The Bride: Kristy bought her dream dress — made of Thai silk, with a beaded bodice and cathedral length train — from a rental shop. It's original value was $1800, she paid only $200! With it, she wore a veil.

The Groom: Aaron rented a tuxedo, which he wore over a Mickey Mouse vest. Instead of a bow tie, he wore a button cover.

Wedding Rings: They bought their rings at a discount jeweler. Kristy chose the interlocking band that matched her engagement ring. Aaron preferred a simple gold band.

The Attendants: Everyone covered the cost of their own clothes. The bridesmaids wore handmade black dresses with boleros; the groomsmen wore plain black pants, white shirts and Mickey Mouse vests. In place of flowers, the bridesmaids carried a brass candle holder with a flower ring and beeswax candle.

Flowers and Decorations: Kristy had her bouquet professionally made, as well as eight corsages and twelve boutonnieres. They were made by the florist at a local grocery store. Because the wedding was held at Christmas, the church was fully decorated. For the reception, which was also held at the church, Kristy's family brought in additional Christmas decorations from their home.

The Ceremony: Kristy and Aaron chose a formal service, conducted by a good friend who is a minister. While they lit the unity candle, the bridesmaids and groomsmen sang. This was followed by a musical tribute from the bride to her parents.

The Reception: The food and drinks were kept simple for the reception. Finger sandwiches, cookies, nuts, mints and wedding cake were served along with coffee and punch.

Photographs and Video: Kristy called a local photography teacher, who recommended one of his former pupils. He charged less than $4 a picture! A video was made by two friends and edited by the groom.

Budget Breakdown:

Marriage License $35
Minister $100
Invitations.. $400
Ceremony Venue $175
Reception Venue $0
Reception Food and Drink...................................... $75
Wedding Cake $140
Decorations $0
Flowers.. $150
Bride's Clothing $300
Groom's Clothing.. $60
Wedding Rings $200
Attendant's Clothing $0
Photographs.. $400
Video $0

Total Cost of Wedding:.................................... <u>*$2035*</u>

In Their Own Words...

During the course of interviewing brides for this book, and in particular this chapter, I heard many wonderful stories and I thank them for sharing them with me. I wish I could have used them all! Instead, I would like to share a few of the featured Budget Brides' quotes with you here:

Kathleen: *"Our wedding was FANTASTIC!!! Truly everything my self and husband wanted."*

Lois: *"Be sensible about spending. The most important part is that two people want to show others their love for one another on this day and for the rest of their lives."*

Kathleen: *"My sister-in-law did the photography and the pictures are more beautiful than if I'd paid tens of thousands of dollars."*

Kristy: *"I bought a beautiful wedding dress. Sure, it had been worn before, but I didn't care. It was my dream dress, and, on top of that, it was cheap!"*

Kathleen: *"We started these plans when we had very little money. Then got a big windfall and could have had a much bigger and more formal wedding if we wanted to — but decided that we didn't want to change a thing."*

Janet: *"Keep it simple and don't worry about what other people think - it's your wedding."*

Kathleen: *"Family and friends agreed that it was one of the nicest and most personal weddings they'd been to."*

And the last word goes to the original budget bride — me! *"Remember, we all enjoyed the wedding of our dreams without paying a king's ransom! You can, too!"*